HELP! I THINK I MIGHT BE

PSYCHIC

101 FREQUENTLY ASKED QUESTIONS ABOUT
SPIRITUAL, PSYCHIC & SPOOKY STUFF

Answered by Helen Leathers & Diane Campkin

ISBN 978-0-9558571-0-2

A catalogue record for this book is available from the British Library.

First Published in 2008 by Spreading The Magic
www.stmpublishing.co.uk

Spreading The Magic, P.O. Box 80, Church Stretton, Shropshire SY6 9AD

Cover Design by Titanium Design Ltd.
www.titaniumdesign.co.uk

www.helpithinkimightbepsychic.com

For anyone who has ever wondered...

Dedicated to
'Petals In The Wind'
who helped us to find our answers.

CONTENTS

ABOUT THE AUTHORS

About Helen

From as far back as I can remember I have seen and communicated with Spirit. Our family home had a number of ghosts, one of which was a wonderful gentle nurse from the early 1900's. When I was four I had had whooping cough, followed by chicken pox, as had my two year-old brother, and much to my mother's horror, my dad also went down with chicken pox. Mum had been up every night for weeks and was exhausted. Then along came what seemed like a miracle, a whole night of uninterrupted sleep. She came in to see me in the morning and said how pleased she was that we had all slept so well. I hadn't, I told her, but a lady in a blue dress had come in and pulled the covers back over me and I went back to sleep after that. Luckily, I do seem to inherit this ability from my mum so although a little perturbed, she mentally thanked 'the lady' for helping out and letting her catch up on some sleep. Many years later my younger sister also saw the lady who appeared to awaken her from a particularly nasty nightmare. She gave a far better description leading us to believe that the lady had been a nurse. 'The Lady', as we now refer to her, obviously continues to care for children in the after life.

Seeing, hearing and sensing ghosts, prophetic dreams and trusting my intuition and inner guidance to avoid potentially negative situations were all a part of my life from very early on. I had devoured all of Doris Stokes books on mediumship well before I was 12. I started reading Tarot when I was 14 and also discovered a natural ability for dowsing with a pendulum. I attended courses and workshops whenever I could from the age of 18 and found a deep affinity with crystals and the native pagan culture of the British Isles. I trained as an alternative therapist and became a Reiki Master. I loved Reiki straight away and knew without a doubt that I had to teach others about it. The self-empowerment, the wonderful healing stories, and the changes that it facilitates in people are all amazing. I started running courses as soon as I could and continue to do so, seeking to make it as accessible to everyone as possible.

Over the years my psychic side became more prevalent and I also realised how empathic I was. I feel the emotions of others, the joy, the fear, and the pain. This can be difficult sometimes but I'm also able to see their potential, which is inspiring. Throughout my twenties I worked closely with friends of like mind, some much more experienced and some at a similar point to me. We discovered more and more about ourselves, our abilities and how to tap into our inner power and knowledge. We debated spiritual philosophy and universal mysteries long into the night. I continued to do card readings and dowsing but also developed other skills including psychometry and Mediumship. I was invited to join a psychic development circle where I met and started working with Diane and others. I found that I was drawn to and had the ability to do 'rescue work'. In layman's terms this is performing something like an exorcism, a horrible phrase conjuring many negative and scary images, but one that most people will understand. Basically I'm good at getting rid of unwanted and problem ghosts. A haunted antique cauldron being the first and most unusual situation that I came across.

At 30 I relocated to Shropshire I found myself with a very definite purpose. I *had* to share my acquired knowledge and understandings with a larger audience. I was running workshops and a website for personal, spiritual and psychic development and had also started writing. Books began to take shape and I knew this was the next step for me.

My journey so far, punctuated by many paranormal experiences, has been a massive learning and development process, and I continue in this every day. I know that I'm connected to the Universe as many seeming coincidences continue to put me in front of the right person at the right time, in a better place, or out of harm's way. I don't consider myself to be special, I have simply chosen to actively pursue this avenue, to open to and connect with the Universe and to develop my own natural abilities, to ask more questions and look for more answers. I enjoy helping others to do the same.

About Diane:

I guess I've always had psychic and spiritual experiences, though for many years I didn't understand them, or even acknowledge them. I had an idyllic childhood, was blessed with a wonderful family, and did well at school, but I always felt different somehow. I didn't feel better than anyone else, nor indeed worse, just different. Perhaps the sensitivity to Spirit around me, strange dreams and even stranger trance experiences that I had, all contributed to my 'feeling different'. That feeling stayed with me until I embraced my spiritual side during my mid 20s, and as clichéd as it may sound, finally found my true self.

My spiritual journey began in earnest when facing upheaval in my personal life. I felt drawn to have a Tarot reading, the first one I had ever had. The cards told an amazing story, describing exactly what I was going through at that time. I was also told that I was a healer, but at that point I had no understanding of what this meant. Upon returning home, my sister jokingly said 'well if you're a healer, heal my headache before it turns into a migraine.' I didn't even know how to go about it, so, between us we kind of guessed that I should put my hands on her head. To our immense surprise her headache did disappear!

My curiosity and a series of amazing synchronicities led me to 'Petals in the Wind', a group that was run by Carol, a Medium and healer. Carol was kind enough to teach me all she knew about healing, and I quickly became a permanent fixture at 'Petals' meetings. I was fortunate to have plenty of time to pursue my new found interests, and over the next few months I went to every workshop I could, joined circles, read books, visited Spiritualist Churches, debated with like-minded new friends – anything that could further my knowledge. It was a time of rapid learning, facilitated by amazing teachers. To this day I remain passionate about teaching people beginning their spiritual journey as a way of returning some of what I was given when I was starting out.

Within eighteen months of my joining 'Petals', Carol moved away and asked me to take over the running of the group. It was an immense honour, if a bit nerve-racking! That was all more than ten years ago now, and although 'Petals' has evolved and changed in many ways since those early days, I'm proud to still be a part of it. I owe a huge amount to my wonderful special fellow members who I always count as my second family. I was also blessed to meet Helen through 'Petals'. Years later we found out that the first time we had worked together we had secretly been in awe of each other. We had both felt nervous as we'd perceived the other to be far more spiritually advanced than ourselves! Interestingly, our great friend Janice predicted that we would work together in a business venture, before she had even introduced us to one another. This book proves her prediction right.

I was also lucky to have Helen become my Reiki Master, passing her knowledge and love of Reiki on to me. My passion for Reiki remains with me and I run regular Reiki courses. I feel privileged to be able to pass on my knowledge of this wonderful healing method to as many people as possible. Additionally I run psychic development workshops with 'Petals', as part of my 'mission' to help people who are exploring their spiritual pathway. Through these workshops I have learnt as much as I have taught.

Over time I have developed many aspects of my spiritual and psychic side, including Rescue work, Angel Card readings, trance mediumship, automatic writing, crystal healing and reading auras to name but a few. I have worked with some amazing Spirit Guides who have patiently helped me along the way! It is a lifelong journey and I am always eager to discover more, and to help others do the same.

INTRODUCTION

Some people believe in 'spooky stuff', others don't. Some really don't care and still more condemn it, at the very least for meddling with things that we don't understand, and at the worst as an act of devil worship. What's very evident, however, is that, generally, people have a strange fascination with the 'unexplained' or 'paranormal', whether they will admit to it or not.

We both grew up having spiritual and psychic experiences from time to time. We also both chose, at a fairly young age compared to some, to pursue our spiritual path and through a series of seeming coincidences found ourselves working together in a development group. Later we began running our own courses and workshops helping others along their spiritual and psychic development journey. We both have experience in providing card and other readings, giving and teaching Reiki and communicating with Spirit, including house clearance and rescue work. For us, seeing, sensing and working with Spirit and unseen energies, including our intuition, is something that we've always done quite naturally. Whilst these phenomena may be 'paranormal', that is, 'supposedly beyond the scope of normal scientific understanding', (according to the Oxford English Dictionary) they're, to us, quite normal. And just to make things clear, we don't actually believe in the devil!

When we mention our interests to anyone, or are running courses, workshops or healing nights, we're often asked questions about our experiences and spiritual philosophies, or conversely we're regaled with stories of spooky goings on and strange scenarios. The questions we're asked usually begin with, "This is going to sound really stupid but...". If we had a pound for every time someone had said those words to us, we would be very rich by now! It never does, by the way. If you want or need to ask a question it's a valid one, never stupid, and we're happy to give our answers. As we've found ourselves answering the same type of questions over and over we felt that there must be many more people who never get the chance to ask someone about their thoughts and experiences in this field. We were privileged to have access to some wonderful teachers and places to learn when we began our spiritual journeys, but for those not so fortunate, our book was born.

In compiling this book we hope to provide everyone with a starting point for those burning questions about healing, personal development, spiritual, psychic and the more spooky matters. We hope that our answers help to clarify some things for you, although it's just a start. We don't claim to definitively know all the answers to everything, nor do we seek to impress our beliefs upon you. We firmly believe that you must always find your own truth. We can tell you what we believe, some of it may resonate with you, and some of it may not, and that's fine. Maybe this book will simply indulge your curiosity and fascination with the unknown, maybe it'll cause you to think about life differently, or to see that it's about more than what goes on in the physical world, as we believe it is. This book could be a springboard for those of you with more than just a passing interest in the paranormal who wish to take your matters further and develop your own skills and abilities. All of these are great reasons to read this book, and we hope it'll provide you with a platform from which you can go on to discover your own personal truth about the wonderful world of Spirit.

When we started this project we decided to take our questions away and write our answers independently. On meeting up to pull our work together for the book we found that, in most cases, we had very similar, if not identical answers. However, occasionally you'll be presented with separate answers from each of us. They may be only slightly different or they may be very different. This is because, despite working together for a number of years, debating our ideas and learning from each other as we've gone along, on some subjects, we have different views. And that's our point, everyone has a different belief structure, and part of ours is that your truth is true for you. But that doesn't mean it's right for the next person, or that theirs is wrong. It doesn't stop us working together and we certainly don't argue over it, much less tell the other she is wrong. How can one human being judge another as being right or wrong over esoteric beliefs and teachings when no one truly knows?

So, in a way, these aren't really answers, they're our take on life's little, and big, mysteries. They're simply our opinions. Please feel free to have your own opinions and enjoy discovering them.

POINTS TO NOTE

Although we talk about communication with Spirit throughout this book, we appreciate that this may be a cause of concern for some people. Our golden rule is always to work with positive and highest intentions. Spirit should never hurt you or encourage you to do anything harmful to yourself or others or to act inappropriately. If at any time you're at all concerned by your experiences you should seek help from an experienced and reputable Medium, healer, or if necessary a medical practitioner.

We often refer to Spiritualist Churches as a point of contact for those interested in or concerned with spiritual matters or psychic phenomena. They will, hopefully, be understanding and sympathetic to your needs or problems. They 'get' the whole Spirit communication thing and should be able to point you in the direction of an appropriate Medium or rescue worker who can help with more serious concerns. They are an option but they're not for everyone. They're, generally, Christian based, so be aware of this if it's an issue for you. They can prove to be very beneficial in pursuing your spiritual path and psychic abilities.

We try to use a capital 'S' to differentiate between 'Spirit', being the non-physical world beyond our own or the 'Higher Realms', and 'spirit' as the essence or soul of a person who has passed, maybe also referred to as a ghost.

HELP! I THINK I MIGHT BE PSYCHIC

SPIRITUAL

I'm really interested in this kind of spiritual and psychic stuff, can anyone do it?

Yes! We believe that everyone has some degree of psychic and healing ability, after all we are Spiritual Beings in human form. And we all use our abilities on a daily basis without even realising it, for example knowing who is on the phone as it rings or sensing the atmosphere in a room where there has just been a row, or even between individuals. If you have ever told a child that you'll kiss or rub their sore hand better you've used your healing abilities on a very basic level. Some people will choose to develop their abilities to a greater extent than others but everyone has them and can tap into them.

Where do I start?

Well what are you most interested in? Are you just interested in collecting and telling ghost stories or do you really wish to develop your own psychic or healing skills? Would you like to learn to read for others through Tarot Cards or similar tools, work with crystals, develop your intuition, see auras, do some form of alternative therapy or healing, communicate with Spirit or learn to see ghosts?

Local groups, Spiritualist Churches, Mediums, the internet etc. can all help you to explore spiritual, psychic and healing matters. The number one tip that we always give people is read, read, read! Books are easily accessible and wide ranging, so plough through as many as you can. As you read and research some elements will resonate with you and you may wish to explore them further. See our 'Top Ten Recommended Reads' at the back of this book. You may find relevant workshops or courses available in your area. You'll also find that if you open your heart to all these new learnings you'll be surprised at what you already 'know' and what you need to explore further. It's up to all of us to find our own personal starting place for our journey, there is no right or wrong. Just enjoy discovering new things.

Having found our own way to where we are now, we felt that there was a need for a tool that really helped people on a practical level in finding out what they're good at and developing their skills in this kind of work. Therefore, we've produced a workbook with in-depth 'lessons' introducing 12 different subjects and including exercises and meditations. If you would like to find out more about this, take a look at the 'Other Products' page at the back of this book.

Do I need lots of expensive equipment?

No! You can develop your abilities very inexpensively. An easy exercise to get you started is psychometry as it utilises the enquirer's own personal items such as jewellery so you can practice your skills on each other. This is, in very basic terms, tuning into and 'reading' any energetic or psychic imprint that has been left by the owner on the item. See the psychometry exercise in Appendix A. You can also make your own 'Angel Cards', Runes and other tools. All it takes is your intuition and a little creativity.

Use the Internet and library to research subjects that interest you. Swap books with friends or take a look in local charity shops or online for bargains. Many local Spiritualist Churches and groups charge nominal fees for workshops on a variety of subjects. Meet with like-minded friends and talk about spiritual matters. Discuss the questions and answers in this book. Do you agree with us? Do you have your own thoughts and theories? You can learn a lot in this way.

I would like to develop my spiritual and psychic side, what one thing can I do?

Helen says: Learn to meditate. Meditation is the single most important skill that you can develop when working in this field. The ability to enter into an altered state of consciousness is key in every other method of development that you'll learn and you'll develop far more quickly if you're able to do this.

The use of meditation for psychic development allows us to enter an altered state of consciousness, by slowing our brainwave patterns, where we disconnect from our rational analytical everyday thinking and reconnect with our subconscious.

Guided meditations can help to develop your visualisation skills and your ability to work with your Guides, gaining information from the other side for yourself and others.

Diane says: Find a spiritual group that you feel comfortable with, who can help you to develop safely. If that's not possible then read anything you can get your hands on. See our 'Top Ten Recommended Reads'.

How do I meditate?

There isn't really as much mystery about this as you might think. Meditation is about being in the moment, not thinking about what you've been up to today, or what you need to do tomorrow. Some people find that they can switch off from all of that when they do something like gardening, jogging, knitting or yoga. The simplest method is to sit or lie comfortably, relax your body and then focus on your breathing in order to clear your mind. The meditation exercise in Appendix B will work through each stage for you. Thoughts and images will come and go, it's impossible to empty your mind completely but you can simply bring your focus back to your breathing should it start to wander.

Guided visualisations are a form of meditation whereby a detailed narrative describes a journey or experience. They will help you not only to relax, but also to begin to visualise in your mind's eye in the same way that you might imagine scenes or images when day dreaming. These can be written by yourself or a friend and read aloud, or they can be bought on CD for specific purposes. You'll find them for sale on the Internet and in good 'mind, body, spirit' shops. Simply sit comfortably and follow them through in your mind's eye. If you wish to do so, you can mentally ask your Angels or Spirit Guides to connect with you and guide you through your meditations.

Look out for meditation groups and evenings where you can find out more. Finally before you undertake any work of this nature ensure you have read the questions regarding 'protection' on page 55 (see also Appendix E).

I'm no good at visualising when I meditate, what should I do?

Practice and persevere. Many people find it difficult to visualise at first, but if you daydream, you can do it! It can take many years of practice. Lots of people only see 'black' when they first start out but in time this gives way to colours and images. Use your imagination. Try sitting comfortably with your eyes shut and re-calling objects or scenes that you're familiar with, for example, your front door, walking around your kitchen, looking at your car, or a favourite place that you've visited. You'll probably find that you start to 'see' your memories of these in your mind's eye. That's the start of it. This is all you need to do when you're following a guided meditation or visualisation. Let the images form in your mind's eye in the same way that a memory does.

When I meditate I see colours, what do they mean?

Colours are one way that we see or sense energy when we work psychically. Different colours have different associations and symbolism. Sometimes their meanings are personal to you and sometimes they're more generic. They can also be linked to the chakras (see the questions on page 24 for more information on chakras), be relative to what you're doing at the time or to a message that you're receiving. Colours may also spring to mind as part of a reading you're doing for someone. Experience and a bit of research can help you to analyse and translate the colours and messages that you're being given. The basic guide to colours in Appendix C is a good starting point.

When I meditate I see eyes looking back at me, what does this mean?

This is a very common experience and, as with most of these subjects, there are a number of theories. Our thoughts are that if you're seeing a single eye, especially if it's large and in the centre of your vision, it could be a symbolic representation of your brow or 3rd eye chakra (associated with psychic and spiritual work) which is being stimulated as you begin working to develop your skills in meditation and other similar activities. It can reveal how 'open' or developed this chakra is. It could also indicate that you've a natural ability or aptitude for clairvoyance (psychic seeing). Eyes in pairs could be those of other souls, perhaps those in Spirit, attempting to connect with or contact you.

Do I have a Spirit Guide?

In a word, Yes! In our opinion, and experience, probably more than one. We believe that everyone has a Spirit Guide(s) either looking out for them, offering some form of unseen protection or guidance (why did you avoid that route home?) or helping out in an area of their spiritual development.

What exactly are Spirit Guides?

Spirit Guides are advanced spiritual beings from higher planes who lend their energy and wisdom in order to help us to evolve spiritually. They're the Spirit World's equivalent of our Mediums. They help us when working spiritually and psychically, but also help by bringing a healing energy to us to restore balance to our lives. They can bring deceased loved ones closer to aid communication, help us to find and pursue our spiritual mission, show us past lives and future potential and act as advisors to groups working together regularly.

We have many different Spirit Guides throughout our life. Some may not even be known to us as yet but still guide and protect us, perhaps speaking through our intuition. There are many people who believe that they've come out of an awful situation miraculously unscathed because a loved one or Angel provided protection, or 'someone' guided them to safety. But that 'someone' is nowhere to be seen after the event. They can be people we've known who have passed on, or family members who we never, or barely, knew. Equally we may not have known them at all in this lifetime. They may show themselves as Angels, children, animals or even mythical creatures. Guides can come and go or be around for different periods in our lives. Even if they seem to have gone they may have just taken a back seat.

Our Guides communicate with us in a number of ways. It might be a thought that magically appears in our minds or a gut feeling to take a particular turning or route. Spirit Guides won't make our decisions for us. This is your life and you must live it. They will communicate opinions and advice if you ask for it, but they won't tell you what to do. Spirit or Spirit Guides should never be used as an excuse by the living; it's always down to you to take responsibility for your own actions.

How do I find out who my Spirit Guide is?

You can be told who they are by Mediums or psychics or even have a drawing of your Guides produced by a psychic artist. However, it's much better to find out for yourself and to develop a relationship and communication channel with them if you wish to pursue your own path of this nature.

Meditation is the best way to discover your Spirit Guide. There are guided visualisations, either in books, or available on CD that are specifically designed to assist you in discovering more about them. You can read books dedicated to the subject or attend workshops and seminars. Of course, you can do it on your own, sitting quietly in a meditative state and asking that they make themselves known to you. Be aware of any subtle changes in the atmosphere or feelings e.g. a touch on the head or a breeze. You may simply have a sense, or feeling of a spirit presence around you. Ask in your mind, "What's your name?" and listen for the first thing that pops into your head. From time to time you may feel that a particular loved one who has passed is around you offering help and protection – they may well be considered to be one of your Spirit Guides.

It can take time and patience to discover your Guides, or it can happen very quickly. However, it isn't actually necessary to know who or what they are, just to have faith that they're there and watching over you. Lots of excellent Mediums don't feel it necessary to know.

Why are all Spirit Guides Native Americans?

They're not! However, this is a common archetypal Guide figure along with nuns, monks and other highly spiritual characters. It seems that those who lived spiritual lives on the earth want to return to help others to achieve their spiritual goals. Native Americans, and other indigenous tribal people, work closely alongside the natural cycles of life, and death, and are very in tune with all aspects of both the physical and spiritual elements of life. In our society we've drifted away from these connections to nature that were essential to their survival. Many believe that their return to us as Spirit Guides is to teach us to reconnect and get back in tune with our natural abilities.

Guides come in many forms and don't have to show themselves in this way. They could just as easily be a young person who appears to be no different to someone you might pass in the street. Guides only take on a form that we recognise because it's easier for us to visualise or understand.

What is the energy that you talk about?

When we're talking about energy we're referring to the 'vital life force' that animates all living things. It has many different names from many different cultures: ki, prana, chi, mana, some will call it God, love, divine source. The list is virtually endless. In order to develop psychically it's important to have at least a basic understanding of some of the theories relating to this energy. It's this energy that we tap into when giving healing, grounding our energy, meditating. It runs through us and connects us all to each other and to the universe. It keeps us alive, well balanced and healthy. It may well even be the essence of our spiritual selves.

What are auras?

In brief, an aura is the energy field that exists around every living thing. It surrounds you three-dimensionally, extending above and below your physical body. Eastern philosophies teach that there are different layers of this energy, each existing at a higher vibratory rate than the previous one.

It's possible with practice and experience to learn to tune into a person's aura and pick up information about it, either visually or simply by 'knowing' or 'sensing'. Information that you may pick up could be the colours in the aura, its strength, any weak spots, imbalances or damaged areas. When we meet other people or go into places or situations our auras are the first part of us that pick up on information in the form of energy. This is then filtered down to our conscious mind for interpretation and action. It's said that when you take an instant dislike to a person or place it's because the energy of your auras aren't compatible for some reason.

The aura can be weakened or inhibited by poor diet, lack of fresh air, lack of exercise, lack of rest, illness, stress, alcohol, drugs, tobacco, negative thoughts or habits or by not protecting yourself sufficiently from external negative influences especially when working psychically. Read the questions regarding 'Protection' in this book (see also Appendix E). A strong healthy aura indicates a strong healthy person and you can work to improve you energy field with a healthy balanced lifestyle and energy work such as Tai Chi and regular meditation.

One interesting point to note is that throughout the ages artists have depicted holy people e.g. Jesus, saints etc. with halos, a representation of their auras perhaps?

Can anyone see auras?

Yes, to some degree and with enough practice. Some people are naturals and have always seen auras around people, animals, and plants, and some people need to work a bit harder. We've taught aura workshops and always had success in helping the most sceptical of students to see auras, even if at the most basic level. If you don't see them on your first attempt, persevere – we really believe that anyone can see them if they're taught how.

How can I start to see auras?

You need to be relaxed and let your eyes gaze around the edge of and just past the person, plant or animal that you're looking at. Your eyes should be slightly out of focus. You'll eventually start to see a blurry glow, almost like a thickening of the air around the subject, just a centimetre or two, as though a heat haze is emanating from them. With practice this will become stronger and you may start to see colours, possibly just flashes at first. Alternatively you may find that you start to sense the colours of the aura, or that the colours just pop into your head.

Initially you may find it easier to practice with someone who works spiritually already, as their aura should be stronger and brighter. It's also easiest to see auras when your subject is standing against a plain background. As you become more adept at seeing auras you may well find that they suddenly appear around people even when you aren't intentionally looking for them.

I can't see auras, is it necessary to see them in order to be able to work psychically?

No it's not. You can work at it, but it's not essential. Some people can feel and sense them instead of seeing them, and this works just as well. If you're starting out, why not begin with something you find easier and you'll probably find that this skill develops as you do.

A friend of mine had a picture of her aura taken, how does that work?

This is known as Kirlian photography or bio-resonance electrography. Basically a picture is taken of you in front of a black background. At the same time your hands are placed on plates with sensors that are positioned at appropriate acupuncture points. A computer is said to pick up the bio-electrical emanations from these points on your hands which correspond to specific parts of the body. It then interprets the frequencies, translating them into colours and superimposing them on to the image of you. The colours and their positions around you are said to mean certain things about what has been going on for you recently and a 'reading' is usually included in the price that you pay so this information will be interpreted for you. Sometimes shapes and images of people, maybe spirits, are seen around you too.

However, some scientists, and the more sceptical, aren't convinced by the technology, maintaining that what's measured is the resistance of a small electric current passed through the plates, the results of which are altered by how much we sweat.

Maybe the pictures are of our auras, maybe they aren't. We've had a number of aura pictures taken over the years, and Helen did start out as a complete sceptic on this subject. What we can both say now is that even if the science doesn't add up on the photography issue, the readings that we've had have all been absolutely spot on. Plus on more than one occasion we've had the colours of our auras read visually by a Medium and subsequently had a picture taken which has been an absolute match. The pictures can be used as tools just as anything else like Tarot Cards, a piece of jewellery and so on can be used by a good reader. Helen has even had a reading off her mobile phone so hey, anything goes if the reader is good!

What are chakras?

Chakras are energy centres within our auras. There are seven major chakras that form a central vertical column following the line of the spine. They're 'wheels' of energy that take in, transform and redistribute energy throughout our energy system. Eastern philosophies teach that in order for us to be whole, healthy, and creative and to continue to develop spiritually, our chakras must be working in harmony with each other, allowing a positive, steady flow of energy.

Each chakra resonates with a specific colour energy which is indicative of its primary functions. There are many less major chakras including the smaller ones in the palms of our hands – used particularly when giving healing, and in the soles of the feet – useful to visualise when grounding our energies.

How do I open and close my chakras and what does this actually mean?

Okay, this is a bit of a misnomer. Our chakras are always open to a greater or lesser degree because they channel the energy which keeps us alive. They can't be closed down – unless we're dead! However, when we work in a way that corresponds with a particular chakra's primary function it opens further. When we work in a psychic or spiritual way we're able to consciously open the higher chakras that relate to this further in order to extend our energies and enhance our abilities. When we're done, we can consciously pull them in again so that we can shut off from working in this way and get back to the physical, otherwise we would be bombarded with psychic energy and impressions all the time. Mostly this is done by visualisation. Eventually you'll be able to tune into your energy and that of your chakras and be more actively involved in this. However, to begin with visualisation works just fine.

What is 'healing' and does it really work?

When we refer to 'healing' it's to the method of channelling energy through a healer to a recipient, usually through the hands, to help restore harmony and balance. This type of healing may be referred to as 'hands on', 'faith', 'spiritual' or 'Reiki' healing. Healing can also be passed on through a touch, a word, a hug or an action, or even being in close proximity to someone. We all know someone that can make us feel so much better just by being there.

Healing can also be sent out to individuals or communities. This is known as 'distance' or 'absent healing' and is also hugely effective. One form of this is prayer.

In very basic terms, our bodies naturally self-regulate, balance and heal themselves but sometimes they don't seem to be able to do this sufficiently and illness or disease occurs. We believe that by channelling healing energy to the individual it helps give them the boost, or 'jump start' to get this mechanism working again.

Does it work? Definitely. And you don't even have to know about it or believe in it to benefit. There's a growing amount of scientific evidence to support the benefits of alternative therapies and healing methods. Below are two excerpts from 'The Field' by Lynne McTaggart[1], which detail the results of careful studies into the effects of healing.

'However, after treatment, those who'd been prayed for had significantly less severe symptoms and required less assistance on a ventilator and fewer antibiotics and diuretics than patients who hadn't been prayed for.'

(R.C. Byrd, 'Positive Therapeutic effects of intercessory prayer in a coronary care unit population', Southern Medical Journal, 1988; 81(7): 826 - 9).

'The results were inescapable. No matter which type of healing they used, no matter what their view of a higher being, the healers dramatically contributed to the physical and psychological well-being of their patients'

(F. Sicher and E. Targ et al., a randomized double-blind study of the effect of distant healing in a population with advanced AIDS: report on a small scale study' Western Journal of Medicine, 1998; 168(6) 356-63)

---

[1] The Field. The Quest for The Secret Force of The Universe by Lynne McTaggart, HarperCollins Publishers 2001

It should be remembered though that whilst healing can be effective on many levels mental, physical, emotional and spiritual, it's not the same as curing. A healer should never diagnose or claim to cure, nor should they prescribe or offer information on anything for which they aren't appropriately qualified.

My hands get hot, cold or tingly in certain circumstances, why is this?

Sometimes this happens to those who are natural healers or who should be pursuing a healing path. Most healers feel heat, cold, tingling or similar sensations in their hands when they're healing. These feelings often occur when someone around you needs some healing energy, not necessarily due to ill health, they may just require an energy boost. It can also happen when you're around other healers or those of like mind.

I have been told that I have 'healing hands' what should I do?

We would recommend that you learn more about the subject and consider doing some development work with healing to help focus your own energy. Start researching in books and on the Internet, you may find that some of your findings resonate with your own experiences. Find a healer or a healing group who would be willing to teach you about healing or perhaps you could take a Reiki course or similar. Healers can be found at local Spiritualist Churches or even working independently from salons or similar, perhaps combining it with alternative treatments such as massage or reflexology. Try local newspapers, phone directories, treatment centres and beauty salons. Best of all is personal recommendation. Always choose to work with someone who you feel comfortable with and are drawn to. You may have to try a number of groups or individual teachers before you find the one that's right for you. Trust your intuition and remember that you'll gain lots of valuable experience along the way.

I have a healing gift, but, as it's a gift, should I charge people for healing?

This can be a very emotive subject and many healers feel strongly that they should never charge people for healing. It's very much a personal decision but bear in mind the following points:

- Unfortunately some people only value things they pay for in today's society, so for some the healing isn't 'real' or 'valid' if it's free.
- You are giving up your time to heal and you may need some recompense for this, even if not for the healing itself.
- You may have had to pay for the training you've undertaken, for example a Reiki course, and you may need to recoup some of those costs.
- You can always exchange something other than money if that makes you feel more comfortable, for example, swap for some gardening, babysitting or even some healing for yourself.

Ultimately you must decide what feels right to you. But if you're even asking the question, the chances are that for every healing session you charge for, you'll give twenty treatments for free!

Are there really such things as angels?

Helen says: The simplest answer to this question is, yes. I believe that there are highly evolved spiritual beings with extremely powerful healing abilities and instant access to universal laws and wisdom. You can feel their powerful energy when they're around and it can only be described as Angelic. Sometimes I receive psychic impressions of Angels which can have a number of interpretations depending on your belief system and what they represent for the person you receive the message for.

Diane says: YES! Angels are everywhere and love to help us if we ask them to. It's probably one of the easiest areas to research because there's so much anecdotal evidence about it. Children seem to be especially receptive to Angelic energy and it's worth encouraging them to connect with their Angels. It's one of my favourite subjects so enjoy discovering about the wonderful Angels all around us.

I keep seeing white feathers everywhere, what's that all about?

Many people, including us, believe that white feathers are the Angels' 'calling cards'. If you notice white feathers, especially really bright white ones, or any in unusual places, the Angels are around you, surrounding you with their love and perhaps letting you know that you're on the right path. If you're interested in connecting with the Angels, ask them to leave you a white feather. They love doing this and one will soon pop up for you.

I keep getting the same events or symbols repeating or showing up in my life over and over again, why is this?

Repeated messages, coincidences and signs around you or in nature, are a nudge from the universe or from Spirit to act in a certain way, or to take action over something specific. It's up to you to take note, decipher the message and then to act appropriately. An example of this is a friend who wanted to develop her psychic abilities but didn't know where to start. She works in a school and her class had a competition to name their new class toy dog. The winning name was 'Petal' which she thought was quite an odd choice. That very same day a friend told her about a development group called 'Petals in the Wind'. She immediately took this as a sign that she should contact the group and quickly became a valued and loved participant in their workshops. So look carefully for repeated messages, signs and coincidences. There will be an important message in them for you somewhere.

A lot of 'new age' shops and therapists have crystals. What are they used for?

Throughout history it has been claimed that crystals are far more than stones or rocks, and that they have metaphysical properties. Each crystal is said to have different properties depending on their make-up and energy. Some of their uses include helping with healing, meditation, manifestation, connecting with Spirit and astral projection. They can be used to heal the mind body and spirit, to provide upliftment and encouragement, to help animals and plants, to purify water, to protect us... the list is endless. We both use crystals and believe that they can have a powerful effect. Here are some of our favourites and their basic uses:

- Amethyst – for enhancing your intuition and psychic ability. Encourages personal development.
- Angelite – to connect with the Angels.
- Black Tourmaline – the best stone for protection and grounding.
- Blue Kyanite – to re-align the chakras.
- Blue Obsidian – great for travellers this stone helps you to find your way.
- Citrine – for abundance, wealth and success.
- Clear Quartz – for enhanced psychic abilities, good health & more energy.
- Jasper – helps you to focus on and deal with earthly matters.
- Pyrite – helps with confidence, revealing deception and getting things done on a practical level.
- Rose Quartz – to attract love, forgiveness, warmth and emotional healing.
- Sodalite – for communication, including with Spirit, helps with mental clarity.
- Tigers Eye – attracts beauty, abundance and practical wisdom.

How do crystals work?

There are a few different theories about how crystals work:

- Crystals 'grow' in and of the earth, forming perfectly uniform structures. This, combined with their chemical composition and colour give each one its own precise vibration. It's said that when something is wrong in our life, whether it's physical, mental, emotional or spiritual, it's because our own energy vibration isn't quite right. By carrying the right crystal or placing it in our energy field our own energy vibration is corrected or brought into line with that which we would like to achieve.
- Crystals, especially quartz magnify energy so they can be used in combination with healing in order to intensify the healing effects on the recipient.
- Crystals are said to radiate their own healing energy in a powerful and concentrated way, much like a 'laser beam'. This can be directed to a specific point where pain, imbalance or disease occurs in order to treat it.
- Another theory is that crystals have a placebo effect and work to facilitate healing because a person believes that they will.

We believe that each theory is a potentially valid one and it may well be that if crystals do indeed have metaphysical properties, an element from each of them could be playing their part. We would suggest that if you want to try them out, do so with an open mind. If you find that crystals are of benefit to you, fantastic! Then decide whether it's important to know how they work or if you can just accept that they do.

How do I know which crystal I need?

There are plenty of books and reference sites on the Internet about crystals so you could look them up and see which one would benefit you depending on your need. However, it's really best to allow your intuition to pick the right one for you. Find somewhere selling crystals and see which one you're most drawn to. Let your crystal pick you! Keep in mind your specific purpose, or ask, in your mind, that you find the one best for you at this moment in time. You may find that by holding them, one feels warm or as though it has a pulse. You could be surprised at the physical reactions and sensations that you receive when handling crystals. Don't try too hard though, even if you pick a crystal simply because you like the colour, it'll be the one that you should have. You can also intuitively choose crystals for friends by thinking of the person in question and again, seeing which crystal you feel drawn to for them. Additionally if you're ever buying crystals for yourself and feel compelled to buy one for a friend, then do so. Start with small tumblestones that you can put in your pocket and keep close to you. These are fairly inexpensive too, so you can try them out without spending much. Please remember that if you suspect that you have a medical problem you should always consult a G.P.

I've been given a crystal by a friend, what should I do with it?

The first thing that you should always do is to cleanse crystals, although you should find out a bit about them first as some can't be cleansed in water. Cleansing is done to shift any energy left by those who have handled it before or absorbed by the crystal from its previous surroundings. Cleansing can be done in a number of ways. It can be held in a flowing stream out in nature, or even under the tap, asking that any negativities be washed away and recycled by the earth into positive ones. You can bury them in a pot of soil or salt (preferably rock salt), or in the garden. Or they can be left in salt water for a few hours. Alternatively, you could simply hold it in your hands asking for it to be cleansed or visualise a cleansing pure white light around it.

Once you've cleansed the crystal you can then dedicate it to serve a specific purpose. For example to help you give up smoking, to help with arthritis and so on. You may simply have been drawn to buy a crystal or not know why your friend has specifically given you it. In these cases you may wish to not dedicate it for any one thing, this is fine too.

You should try to recharge your crystals regularly. This can easily be achieved by leaving them in the sunlight, moonlight or rain for a few hours (again, beware of porous crystals). Crystals love thunderstorms and seem to be especially charged up after being left outside during one.

What you do with crystals generally depends on the type, size and shape of them. This is a very basic starting point for you:

- Crystal pendants and other jewellery are a great way to carry crystal energy with you wherever you go.
- Tumblestones can be put in a small pouch and kept in a pocket or handbag. They're used for healing, energy work or divination.
- Crystal balls look great as an ornament, are used for scrying and will enhance the energy of a room.
- Natural points or shaped wands are specifically used for healing and chakra work
- Pendulums can be used for healing, chakra work and dowsing.
- Clusters, caves and geodes are often used for decorative purposes. They radiate positive energy into and absorb negative energy from their environment. Also, they're said to be good for cleansing or can be a focus during meditation.

Finally, and most importantly, enjoy your crystals. You may well find that you end up with a large collection!

How can I find my soul mate and how do I know when I've found them?

Helen says: By 'soul mate' most people mean lover, life partner, spouse or similar. I tell anyone searching for that special 'someone' that they must stop looking. I don't mean stay at home and never go out, you do have to be out there to meet people. No, I mean that you have to be happy with yourself and who you are first. Absolutely content with being on your own. If you don't love yourself, how can someone else love you? You have to work at it and it can be difficult but that's my best advice and advice that has come up and been borne out for others over and over again in readings. How do you know when someone is your soul mate? Oh, I'm afraid it's that really vague answer, 'you just do'. Sorry, but there's no other way to describe it. How can you describe love? It's impossible. But aside from feelings, a true soul mate will love you no matter what, not judge you, and not hurt you in any way or on any level. They will respect you and let you be the person you are now, but also allow you to grow into the person you must become. They will never seek to own or control you. They will want for you what you want for you, so long as it's not harmful of course. And if you're soul mates, you'll want the same for them.

Diane says: This is a subject much open to debate. For my part, I believe that we often have more than the traditional sole soul mate. I believe that in the Spirit Realm we're all part of a large group of souls within the whole, and that we often choose to incarnate with some of our soul group. This is why we sometimes feel especially drawn to someone, be it a partner, or a friend.

We come from the Spirit World that's pure love, and once in our earthly incarnation we constantly seek that pure love on a subconscious level. Consequently many of us feel a desperate need to connect with a 'soul mate' i.e. another soul who can help us to recapture that feeling. We often mistake that need for a feeling that our soul mate is somehow our 'other half' who can make us whole. I truly believe that we can't achieve this level of fulfillment through another person; we have to find it within ourselves. When we accept this, the constant striving to find our mystical soul mate becomes less important, and instead we can enjoy our relationships with other members of our soul group when we come across them, in a more realistic and grounded way that will ultimately bring us more happiness. Soul mate relationships can be wonderful, but please remember it's just as important, and can bring just as much joy, to live your life without them.

I want to have a card reading to find out about my future and to help me make the right decisions. How should I go about this?

If you're looking for a reader it's always best to go on a personal recommendation if you can. Ask friends, family or work colleagues if they've had a good reading with anyone. If not, go along to a psychic fair and choose a reader that you feel drawn to. Or visit a Spiritualist Church where they could put you in touch with someone. However, readings should only give you an overview of your options, and guidance. You shouldn't base decisions on or rely solely on another person's interpretations of messages or personal situations. Your decisions are yours, and yours alone. Guidance and an overview can help to clarify things but at the end of the day, your life is your own responsibility.

Is there any truth in this 'cosmic ordering' stuff?

Most definitely yes! Along with magic and spells, healing and prayer, cosmic ordering is a powerful tool that's available to us all as creative beings. Cosmic ordering can help us to manifest the things we desire for our higher good.

As each thought we have is energy and energy creates everything, it makes sense to us that creating good energy will create good things. Decide what it is that you wish to achieve, be specific, have a clear picture of it in your mind and put the thought out to the universe that you'll receive it, and be thankful in the knowledge that you will. Read up on the subject and give it a go for yourself (see our 'Top Ten Recommended Reads'). Diane has a great example of how cosmic ordering worked for her and her family and how you have to be careful and specific about what you order.

"My husband was facing redundancy, so I 'ordered' him a new job, asking that he be better paid in his new employment, and receive a company car, both of which would be beneficial to our family life at that time. I stated the ideal location for his new job, and the working hours. He rapidly gained new employment and all of the items on my wish list were fulfilled. Unfortunately the job was very stressful. My husband felt constantly taken advantage of despite working extremely hard, and even worse, after a year he was facing redundancy again. This time I was more careful with my requirements. As well as the list I had previously set out I added that I wanted him to work for a company that really appreciated his ability and hard work. Again he quickly secured a new job that fitted all of the original criteria. Better still, within three months of joining he had received a company award which recognised individuals who have gone beyond the job they're contracted to do for the benefit of the company and their clients, thus proving that they were a company that really did appreciate his efforts!"

How do I know what my 'life purpose' is?

We get asked this question so many times. The only answer is, don't worry about it. Many believe that your life purpose is simply to live and experience a physical life, so why not start there? Make it the best life you can. Be happy and enjoy it. If you feel that there's more that you want to do with your life and you should be taking on something specific, then try new things. If it's spiritual or psychic work that you're drawn to then have a go at some of the ideas mentioned in this book. Go to a meditation group, meet people of like mind or learn a new skill. You may find you're initially drawn to one thing, such as healing, but then this leads you to another, such as card readings. Eventually you'll find something that really resonates with you and it'll naturally become your main focus.

You don't have to restrict yourself to one type of work and it doesn't even have to be of a psychic nature. Be open-minded. It may be that your life purpose isn't what you expect. It could be anything from teaching, entertaining, physical fitness, inspirational speaking or looking after animals to being a great parent. The key is to enjoy your spiritual journey as you seek your 'higher purpose'.

Think about what you enjoy doing, what makes you smile or feel content? This is a good indication that it's something you should be doing. Also take a look at the things that you dislike and wish to change in the world. Combine these two elements so that you find a way to use what you love doing to initiate change for the better. Artists are brilliant at this as they have a public platform to express their messages of concern over hunger, poverty, abuse and even politics. As less public figures we may not hold as much sway with large audiences but we can make small positive changes on a daily basis in our local community, or even in our own home. This is a great place to start.

When you feel that you've connected with your life purpose you can begin to act upon it. This is amazingly liberating and fulfilling and we hope that all of you, who wish to, do so.

Are our life plans set in stone or is everything down to fate? Do we have any influence over what happens to us?

Helen says: This is a really tricky subject and one that your opinion is likely to change on as you proceed through life, depending on what's going on for you. I believe that we're here to experience living, but also to remember that we're creative and a part of the divine. I do think that we each have a role to play in life and that we've probably agreed it or worked it out before we got here. But how we go about achieving our 'higher purpose' is up to us when we get here and subject to our interactions and experiences with others. We often can't remember what our 'higher purpose' is, which is why we have to listen and watch for signs to point us in the right direction. I always believe that everything happens for a reason. Some things you can change and some you can't. The hardest part is knowing which is which! We always have a choice in everything that we do, and we can also choose how to react to events that appear to happen to us through no fault of our own. It's really hard sometimes but it is possible. I would say to anyone who feels like their life isn't in their control that you should step up to the challenge, work on yourself and your thoughts. You are a creative being and you can take control.

Diane says: A huge subject that even now, I still find difficult to answer! I think that we do draw up a blueprint before we incarnate setting out the lessons that we wish to learn in this lifetime, and the challenges that we have to undertake in order to learn these lessons. We then incarnate and meet our obstacles and either learn the lessons from them or don't. If we don't, I believe that another similar set of circumstances presents itself, and these patterns continue until we finally learn what we were supposed to learn. So, yes, we do have influence over what happens to us, especially in how many times we have to keep meeting the same-themed challenges. I truly believe that in life, what's important isn't what happens to us but how we deal with what happens to us, and I always try to live my life by that mantra.

Do you believe in reincarnation and past lives?

This is a massive, complex and emotive subject. It's the sort of subject that, because we've no definitive answer, has to be down to your personal thoughts. As with all matters of this nature, what rings true for you? That will be your truth until such time as it changes. You may experience something in the future that makes you rethink your opinion on this, and that's fine. Your truth is what you believe it to be. However, for those of you who don't know what your truth is right now, here are our thoughts on it. We hope that they help. Even if you disagree with our thoughts, at least you'll know what you don't believe and sometimes that's half the battle.

Helen says: I believe that 'past life' is simply a term for a seemingly familiar vision of an alternate reality or life experienced in the first person. From this vision we can gain intimate access to universal information or lessons. This experience can occur in the form of dreams, meditation or similar. I have had experiences which appear and feel to be 'past life experiences'. They've helped to explain some of my feelings towards certain things, my interests, how I 'know' someone and why I have acted in a particular way. But I don't think that we're born, live, die, hang around in heaven for a bit until we fancy being reincarnated again, then come back here to go through it all again. I believe that it only seems that we come to earth more than once because we're under the illusion that we're all individuals, when we're actually all one, all a part of life, or the universe, or god. Different 'parts' of us have different experiences of life. We're able to tap into a big pool of information or energy and retrieve relevant information, about our other 'parts' that will help us with a given situation. A bit like the way a friend may relate a similar situation that they found themselves in, in order to help you understand and deal with your own situation better. However, sometimes we accidentally get glimpses of an event the 'other parts' are experiencing without knowing why, similar to getting a crossed line on the telephone. Because we're truly all one, they feel as though they're a part of us and we experience them as a 'past life'. I believe that time isn't linear (although we perceive it as such) so this information could be from any event at any time in the past, present or future. We are, therefore, also able to communicate with anyone who has lived, lives in the physical world now, or will do in the future, which also helps me explain mediumship.

This can be really hard to get your head around, as a part of all of us is effectively everywhere and in every moment, at once. I found that reading the 'Conversations with God' series by Neale Donald Walsch really helped me and made it feel relatively simple to understand. You may find that you need to read this answer more than once!

Diane says: I have read and also experienced many things that make me believe in the essence of reincarnation and it's something that resonates strongly with me. It's a truly fascinating subject which I'm continuing to explore and intrigues me further when I look into the subject of time and begin to wonder if all our many lives are playing out alongside each other at the same time.

Do you think that you go to hell if you're a bad person?

No. We believe that beyond the physical world there's the Spirit World and that there's no differentiation between 'good' and 'bad' people. However, as spiritual beings we believe that there must be a process at some point, maybe following physical death, by which we gain an insight into our impact on others during our lifetime. This would be the ultimate in 'what goes around comes around' whereby you would experience all that you 'gave out' in your physical lifetime. Consequently, for some, creating their very own hell. Of course, people have free will to act in whichever way they see fit and they act appropriately according to their belief system, their view of the world and their frame of reference. If we're given free will but are then judged on it by a god, and sent to heaven or hell, do we really have free will at all? That's like saying to someone, you can believe what you want, but if it's different to what I believe you'll be punished. The series of books, 'Conversations with God' and the follow up, 'What God Wants' by Neale Donald Walsch really helped us to begin to work out our thoughts on this very difficult and emotive subject.

As for the devil as a factor in evil doings, well, as humans, don't we just love to place the blame and make excuses? So if we don't understand something, can't place the blame at someone else's feet, or won't take responsibility for our own actions then we seek an outside influence, which is where demons, or the devil come in!

Do you believe in God?

We always say that we do believe in god, with a small 'g'. Basically we believe in a single divine creative force, whether it's called God, Allah, Goddess, Love, whatever. We also believe that we're all a part of god and that god is within us. In this way, all of creation is connected. We don't personally hold with the confines and dogma of organised religion and struggle with the damage and harm that has been, and unfortunately continues to be done in the name of any religious institution. However if it works for another then we're happy for them. So long as they've made their own mind up and continue to challenge and assess what's being told to them by another human being rather than simply accepting everything. As with this book, don't take anyone's word for anything, especially something as personal and intangible as belief and faith. You have to 'feel' and find your god for yourself.

PSYCHIC

Help! I think I might be psychic but my friends and family just say that I'm weird and it's a load of rubbish. What should I do?

Firstly, the most important piece of advice we can give is for you to find your own truth. We're all individuals, at different stages in our spiritual development and leading different lives. Some people do believe all this stuff is nonsense and we respect their right to that opinion. Our own experiences tell us that, for us, it's not nonsense, but that's *our* belief. So you should feel free to investigate the subjects that interest you. Work with the ones that resonate with you, respect other peoples' opinions even if they're different to your own, and never try to force your opinions on others. You must pursue your own truth or you'll never be the person that you could be.

Secondly, what do you want to do? If you don't want to take things further and develop your psychic potential then you can learn to shut out any such experiences that you may be having. Read the questions regarding 'Protection' in this book (see also Appendix E).

If you do want to develop your skills further then you need to seek people of like mind. Your local Spiritualist Church could be a good starting point for you. They usually have regular meetings and evenings of clairvoyance that you can go along to. They're very welcoming and will be able to tell you about courses, workshops, and development circles that they or others run locally. Be aware, however, that they're usually run from a Christian background, so if this is an issue for you it may not be your best option. It just depends what you wish to gain from the experience. You can also look for local workshops and courses, meditation groups and similar. Go along to a local psychic or 'mind, body spirit' type fair, or look for adverts in gift shops, crystal or 'new age' and health food shops, libraries and alternative health clinics. We should mention that the same caution should be exercised when meeting people through these networks as through any other. Just because they're attending a spiritual event does not mean that they're automatically safe to be with. As always use your own common sense and judgement.

When you start doing this you may wish to keep it to yourself if people around you aren't supportive. Once you find people of like mind and start attending events you may find that you can join a group or open circle, or even start something up yourself, or with your new found friends. Once you start to develop your skills and confidence you'll probably find that you can ignore the comments of others as you begin to prove things to yourself. Do be wary of attempting to prove others wrong however, as this can appear a bit desperate and ego-centred. It's far better to let things go along at their own pace and gradually you'll begin to gain their respect. Also be aware that as you gain confidence and find your own spiritual path people can begin to fall by the wayside. Some don't like their friends or family to change. It's too much of a challenge for them and causes too many questions about their own life. Try not to enter into heated debates as this can cause more conflict. Sometimes you just need to walk away knowing that you're doing what's right for you. In fact, a level of emotional detachment is a skill that's essential to develop as you continue to work in a psychic way.

I often know who is on the phone before I answer it, am I psychic?

This doesn't apply if you have 'caller ID'! You're basically tapping into your innate intuition. It could be that it's always a person that you have a really great rapport with, or a relative and your close connection means that you have a telepathic or sometimes empathic link. Parent/child and siblings, especially twins, are the most common relationships to have this link. It's certainly good that you recognise that this happens to you and indicates that you could do well if you want to develop your psychic abilities further.

How do I know if I have a gift?

Everyone has a gift of some sort but some choose to develop their abilities more than others. It could relate to psychic abilities, healing qualities, Spirit communication or a natural skill at reading cards or using a similar tool. If you're even asking this question it's likely that on some level you're looking to develop your own abilities in one of these areas. Give it a go and see how you get on. Be aware of your own intuition as you go about your daily life and you'll soon realise that you do have a gift and are already using it to some extent. As you give it more attention it'll become greater. Attend development workshops or open circles and see what happens. Working with others will help to give you feedback and validation and boost your confidence.

Sometimes things just pop into my head. How do I know I'm not making it up?

This is a difficult question to answer and it comes up over and over again when people begin to develop their skills. If we could answer this one definitively, we would be very rich!

It's normal to feel that you may be making stuff up or imagining it, especially when trying out new techniques such as card readings, psychometry and dowsing. All you can do is acknowledge the thoughts and trust your intuition about them. As you practice you'll learn when the information you're receiving is from your intuition, Spirit Guides, or psychic self and when it's your own imagination or mind, perhaps wishful thinking. The thoughts that are quite random or that spring to mind when you're asking a question are usually the ones from Spirit. And in relation to working psychically, such as when practising psychometry, you should always pass on any information that you pick up on, or receive, right from the start no matter how silly or trivial it sounds. If you're right you'll receive positive feedback from the person you're reading for. In some instances however, information given in a reading can't be confirmed straight away so you'll not know for sure then and there. In other instances the information may be refuted entirely.

With experience you'll be able to filter out what's 'you' and what's information from 'them'. There's a subtle difference but it takes time and experience to figure it out. You need to develop confidence in your abilities. We always feel that some doubt is preferable to over-confidence, which can cause some people to become or appear to be egotistical.

Can you interpret my dreams?

Sometimes we've used our psychic abilities to decode dreams for people, however we also tell people that they can interpret their own dreams successfully and accurately themselves.

We believe that as we receive messages from both our subconscious and Spirit, dream interpretation can be a very useful tool at our disposal. Firstly, it's important to work out if the dreams are actually 'telling' you something or are your mind's way of processing stuff. Dreams are very personal and can be affected by lots of outside influences. For example, stress or worries can manifest in your dreams, what you experience during the day or what you've seen on the TV, certain types of food, caffeine or alcohol can all affect your dreams. So use your common sense to discount the elements of your dream that may have been influenced by such factors, and then use your intuition to decode the rest.

A dream analyst or dream dictionary may suggest certain generic symbolic associations while they may mean something else entirely to you. Plus, have you ever tried to tell your dream to someone else? You may be able to tell the story to a degree, but you can never translate the emotions or feelings that the dream gives you. Therefore asking others to interpret a dream for you can be a starting point, but lots of other elements have to be taken into consideration so you're probably the best person to decipher them. If you wish to interpret your dreams on a regular basis it's worth investing in a diary in which to record your dreams on waking. Set your alarm clock ten minutes earlier to have time to do this. You'll find that the more you do this, the more of your dreams you'll be able to recall.

Sometimes I dream that something bad is going to happen, how do I stop this?

Unfortunately this does happen to some people. The best advice we can give is to learn about psychic protection (p.55), ask your Guides, Angels and loved ones in Spirit to watch over you and surround you while you sleep, and ask them to stop the dreams that you don't like or want. You may find that by constructively channelling your natural abilities which are currently manifesting in the form of prophetic dreams, it'll help to prevent them, or at least let you have more control over them. We would suggest beginning a course of spiritual and psychic development and to ensure that you put protective measures in place while working and that you close and ground your energies afterwards (see Appendices D & E).

Sometimes I dream that something bad is going to happen. What should I do with the information?

This is tricky. Some people believe that everything happens for a reason. This invites the question, should we interfere? But then again, aren't we given the information for a reason? If we aren't meant to take action, why do we get it? We could talk ourselves around in circles over this.

We say if we're meant to intervene it'll be possible for us to do so in some way that will have an effective outcome. Do you feel compelled to take action, and is it a realistic undertaking?

Sometimes we may be given the information as confirmation of our connectivity with everything and a concept of a 'bigger picture'. As with most things of this nature, it's essential to go with your own gut instinct on this. You may feel that it's appropriate for you to tactfully pass warnings on to friends or family members. Remember, though, that people may not welcome warnings or bad news.

We don't feel that dreams of death should be relayed. This is because there may well not be a way to alter the outcome of a given situation. There's no guarantee that your dream is accurate, and at the end of the day, we all have to go at some point. Dreams can also take some interpretation. A death in a dream could be as symbolic as the 'death' card in Tarot which represents an end, and inevitable start of something new.

If you feel that you're receiving information about forthcoming events or that could help with a current situation, such as a crime or missing person, what should you do? We know that there are people who have gone directly to a person, or the authorities involved with such cases, and given over the information that they've received, and this is certainly an option for you. Whether they will act on it is quite another matter. However, in order to give some credibility to your findings it would be useful for you to have some form of documented evidence of previous situations in which you've received accurate information. Keep a journal and record any information that you receive about any news item or possible future event. This might be through dreams, gut reactions or feelings whilst watching a news item or something that comes through to you during a meditation or reading. Ensure that every detail is recorded and dated, and, if possible witnessed. If you work in a group, you may wish to start a group journal – remember to record who receives the information next to each entry. When anything comes up that confirms your information, put this in the journal alongside the original entry or cross-reference it to an 'outcome' file. Be prepared that for many of your recordings, you may never get an answer. If you do find that you have continuing accuracy and good confirmation and you do wish to approach anyone about future findings you can use your journal to encourage them that you've a track record. Be wary, some people may be desperate for information and see you as a saviour. Don't get personally involved and don't over-promise.

Why don't I ever get dreams about good stuff?

You probably do but are less aware of them as they're usually less eventful and impactful. Think about it, you're far less likely to remember a dream where the driver of a car stopped to let you cross the street than one where a driver nearly runs you down. This is because the emotions and physical reactions, even during a dream, are going to be far greater in the 'bad' dream than the 'good' dream.

I had a dream about my deceased loved one and it felt so real. Did they really visit me?

Helen says: If you feel as though your loved one has visited you, then yes, they have. And if anyone questions you to the contrary, tell that person to prove that they didn't. Who defines what's 'real' and what isn't? It's all a matter of perception.

Diane says: The key words here are 'it felt so real'. If you've had a dream of a loved one that feels very real, vivid, or like it's more than a dream, then it almost certainly was a spirit visiting you. Our loved ones in Spirit do enjoy coming to visit us and seem to find it easier to do so while we're sleeping.

While we often dismiss these experiences as simply wishful thinking on our part, visitation dreams stand out as markedly different. As well as the feeling of 'realness' already mentioned, it's also possible to experience physical sensations such as a touch or a hug, and this sensation can still be felt when you wake up. Sometime no verbal communication takes place within the dream. Communication is either telepathic or unnecessary as you and your loved one are simply content to be reunited. Commonly the dreamer will say to their loved one, "but you're supposed to be dead", which luckily never seems to offend them! Another big clue that can help you to identify a spirit visitation is the immense emotion that follows it. Upon waking you can clearly remember, in great detail, what happened during the experience, and the memory can often move you to tears, both immediately after and upon subsequent retelling. Finally, if you wish to receive a dream visitation from a loved one, take a moment before you go to sleep one night to ask them to visit, either mentally or out loud. But be patient, it may be some time before this happens.

How do Mediums get messages from Spirit and what do they mean when they say they 'see' things?

Mediums get messages by channelling information from Spirit. They act in the same way that a radio receiver does by tuning into their specific frequency in order to receive 'spiritual broadcasts'. These 'broadcasts' are then received by the Medium in a number of ways. The main ways are:

- Clairaudiency - which is translated as 'to hear clearly'. Some people are able to hear messages from spirits and Guides either in their 'minds ear' or audibly as though someone is actually speaking to them.
- Clairvoyancy - which is translated as 'to see clearly'. Most 'see' with their mind's eye, but some are able to physically see spirits, symbols and messages that need to be passed on to others.
- Clairsentiency - which is translated as 'to sense clearly'. Most Mediums work, in all or part, in this way. It's often a case of 'knowing', or having a sense of something that's being passed on from Spirit. This seems to be the most common method of working. It's arguably the easiest skill to develop yet the hardest to explain.

Use of terms such as 'I sense', 'I see', I feel', 'I'm being given or told', or 'They're telling me' are usually indicative of the Medium's most dominant sense when working psychically.

Other methods of communication also exist and all of these can be developed with work. Some people will be aware of scents that are manifested by a spirit to announce their presence. This can be very powerful as the centre in the brain associated with smell is so close to our memory centre that smells and memories are often intricately linked. Some people find that they get a certain taste in their mouth that's associated with the spirit or is important to the person that they've come through for. Another method of Spirit communication is automatic writing. Some Mediums will find that they can draw pictures with the help of their Guides, or that they write messages for themselves or others. We believe that we received a lot of Spirit help while writing this book, parts of which we don't recall having written at all!

Why don't Spirit give us information in words and sentences? Why do we get abstract symbols?

We get so frustrated by this at times too. Basically, it seems that Spirit communicate through a telepathic process and don't really use words as we do. It's not easy to establish communication between the different planes. They have to transmit down to us from the higher realms and it may be that it's quicker and easier to send symbols, plus it's said that our own subconscious understands symbols better. So they use them, along with feelings and sensations. Think about it, if I were to mention that we were going to have a fruit salad tonight, more than likely you would think of a dish of fruit salad in the form of a picture, seeing the pieces of fruit: melon; apple; orange; and so on. You wouldn't see or hear a list of all the ingredients literally being spelled out to you. So, you think in pictures. Additionally, if we're receiving information to pass to others, oftentimes symbols are enough for the recipient because they have a personal meaning to them. And, it's not always appropriate for someone else's business to be spelt out to us. It can be tricky, however, as we have to learn to translate what they're giving us and our human, analytical side can get in the way. Our 'logic filters' can confuse the messages that we receive so once again, practice and perseverance are essential.

I really want my deceased loved one to talk to me but they never come through when I have a reading, why not?

Firstly, no Medium should claim to definitely be able to contact a specific loved one for you. They've no way of knowing that. Communication is a two-way process and your loved one has to want to come through, they can't be made to. Sometimes it can take a long time to establish communication with a loved one however desperately you want it. We believe this is because Spirit know when we're truly emotionally ready to hear from them. However much you think that you're ready, they really do know best and they won't come through until they think it's right for you. Finally if you've only tried with one Medium it may be worth trying with another. Your loved one may find it easier to communicate through a different Medium, no matter how good the first one is.

How long must a person be 'in Spirit ' or deceased before they can 'come through'?

There are many different opinions about this. Mediums will give you different answers for this based on their experiences. We've found that they can come through very quickly, within hours even, however, this isn't very common. They may need to practice their new forms of communication. Early contact may be very brief because of this but should improve over time as the spirit becomes more 'experienced'. As we mentioned before we believe that Spirit know when we're truly emotionally ready to hear from them and they may wait longer to allow us to deal better with the physical separation that we experience when a loved one passes.

Someone has told me it's wrong or evil to speak to the dead. What do you think?

This is often said by churchgoers, priests etc. Of course, they're entitled to their own opinion as much as we are to ours and it's up to you to make your own mind up about this. It's a highly emotive subject. Our own experiences are that spirits love to communicate with us as much as we're fascinated by them. They especially love that they can help to reassure us that they live on and are okay. If that reassurance brings comfort to those left behind by their loved ones, we don't see how that can be a bad thing. If a spirit is earthbound and unable to move into the light and on to the Spirit Realms, then we believe that they should be helped and encouraged to do so. After all, if we saw a person lost in the street, we would give them directions. We've never received any information during our dealings with Spirit to suggest that communicating with them is harmful to them or us in any way, in fact, quite the opposite.

We've never courted the attention of or 'summoned' Spirit. They made their presence known to us and then we chose to develop our abilities in order to help others as we felt very strongly that was our pathway in life. We work in love and light always and our opinion is that we work with and for a higher good.

When children cross over do they stay as they are or do they grow up in Spirit?

In our experience, once a spirit has crossed and while they remain in the Spirit Realms, they revert to a Spirit or light body. This is an essence that no longer resembles human form and as such isn't governed by the ageing process or any physical restrictions.

However, in order for us to easily recognise them when they visit, for example through a reading with a Medium, they show themselves in the form that will be most familiar to us. So if they passed at age 8, they'll be seen as they were at that age. They'll also show themselves in full health in order to reassure loved ones that they're now free from pain and suffering. They may however show the Medium the physical reasons for their passing to validate who they are.

On occasions they may also come through as older, if they believe it's necessary for their loved ones to be given proof that they're truly happy and have moved on. They'll still be recognisable as they retain their own unique energy which will be familiar to their loved ones.

Either way the children who we've communicated with are always happy and content to be in the Spirit World, with their only concern being for their grieving families.

If you have two loves in your life who do you go to when you cross?

This is such an important question to so many people, and the good news is that you can go to both of them! In our Spirit form we don't have the same human emotions that would create a complex situation where we would have to choose. We don't love in a sexual nor a jealous way, rather our souls are all a part of a whole, and as such we'll be overjoyed to reunite with all of those that we've loved in our earthly lifetime.

I can't read tarot (or use another specific tool). It's so frustrating, what can I do?

You have two options, either,

- Try something different. Either a different style of Oracle Card or a completely different tool. Helen learnt to use Tarot when she was 14 and used them for years but Diane connected far better with 'Angel Cards' and finds them easier to use despite repeated attempts at the Tarot. Now we both use 'Angel Cards' out of preference. Neither of us are any good at crystal ball readings so we found other tools that we work better with. And very often, with luck and practice you don't need any tools at all.

Or

- Practice and persevere: While some are lucky enough to pick up a tool or technique and run with it, mostly we need to develop our skills. Like anything that we do in life we need to learn, understand, practice and develop.

Is it true that you should only use Tarot cards that someone else has bought for you?

Many people say this is true, but in our opinion it really doesn't matter. We often advise people to buy themselves a Tarot or Angel card pack that they feel drawn to as we believe that they will work better with a pack chosen intuitively. Helen's first set of Tarot Cards were given to her by her mum when she was 14 years old. Her mum had been using the set herself for years but that fact never got in the way of Helen's readings and she continued using them for over

10 years. We've both bought packs for ourselves and again, there have been no problems when using them.

As with many practices, over the years, complex rituals have evolved over the usage of Tarot Cards, e.g. that they should be kept wrapped in black silk, no-one else should ever handle your cards, when you give a reading there's a particular set of things the enquirer should do regarding shuffling, splitting the pack and so on. Our personal view is that these rituals are often unnecessary and not following them does not stop the cards working. If you can read the cards, you can read the cards. However, we do respect that for some, it's important to adhere to age-old traditions or rituals. As we've said in previous answers, follow your instinct and find a way of working that resonates with you.

I sometimes read cards or palms after I've had a few drinks. Is that ok?

A big resounding NO! Please don't do this. Our number one rule is to NEVER mix your spirits! We know many people do because they think it's fun and harmless, or because they're actually really good at it but have no confidence ordinarily, but please don't. There are two reasons for this. Firstly, it lowers the protection around you and you can attract unwelcome energy by doing this because your guard is down. Read the questions regarding 'Protection' in this book (see also Appendix E). Secondly, we have a responsibility when giving readings to take care of how we pass on sometimes personal and sensitive information. As we all know, drink lowers our inhibitions making it less likely that we will pass it on tactfully.

I hear voices in my head, am I going mad?

First and foremost, if you ever hear voices that urge you to do bad things or to harm yourself or others, please seek medical advice. It's our experience and belief that Spirit communicates with us telepathically, i.e. in our heads. As long as the above doesn't apply, then we believe that you're unlikely to be going mad! Try to find a reputable Medium or development group who can help you to work with your psychic ability, or, should you wish, to stop it happening.

What happens if you get something bad about a person during a reading?

If you're providing readings for others, using cards, dowsing, psychometry or other means, you have to do so responsibly. Be cautious when giving out information or interpretations for others, and take great care and consideration before passing on any negative information. Generally it's not recommended to give bad news to anyone, as you've no idea as to how accurate your information is or what effect it'll have on the enquirer. You have to use your intuition and your common sense. We find that, with experience, you'll know how and when to give this sort of information, if at all. If you're training under the guidance of a more experienced reader have a chat with them and seek their advice on this. Sometimes it can be very difficult to keep such information to yourself, but if you're ever in any doubt, keep quiet!

Can people really dowse for water?

Dowsing is the practice of using a device such as a stick, L-shaped rods or a pendulum to find a person place or thing, or the answers to yes/no questions, indicated by the device's movements. Traditionally a dowser holds a Y-shaped hazel twig horizontally out in front of them, parallel to the ground. A downward movement of the twig would indicate water below the ground.

Throughout history there are many documented cases of dowsing being used to find both water and oil. It's easy enough to try dowsing for yourself you just need to focus on what you're looking for or the question that you need to know the answer to.

If you're psychic, what are the lottery numbers?

LOL! How many times have we heard this one? If we knew this we would be sunning ourselves on a beach right now.

Helen says: Life and time are complex. Every single thing that occurs in any given moment can affect the outcome of every other moment. Some people do get given information about lottery numbers, winning horses etc. and quite possibly at that given moment, that information could be correct. But as we all impact on each other's existences, in the next moment, something may have changed, or it may not have done! Also, think about it, if every psychic got the lottery numbers, there wouldn't be much of a share of the jackpot for each one. We believe that it's possible to achieve everything we want, or to manifest items or events in our lives but you have to be really in control of all your thoughts, especially your own negative programming and subconscious restrictions – and this is a subject for another day, possibly another book!

Diane says: Spirit have far more important messages to communicate, and of course not everyone can win the lottery, so we can't all be given the winning numbers. Winning the lottery is a life-changing experience and if it's not part of our 'life-plan' (decided, I believe, before we incarnate) we won't be given the numbers.

I want to do psychic work, but I'm scared of actually seeing anything, should I give up?

NO! You don't have to experience anything that you don't want to or aren't ready for. Simply state to your Guides that you don't wish to see anything yet. In, fact, actually seeing a physical form is rare and quite advanced. Most people start by sensing and feeling things (clairsentience) and work their way up to seeing in their mind's eye. As you gain in confidence you may find that you no longer feel scared. Also if you do physically see something, it's usually quite mundane and unassuming and it's often only afterwards that you think, "Oh, I think I may have seen a ghost!"

I don't want to go into a trance, be possessed, be taken over or have someone else speak through me. How can I stop this happening?

You never have to do anything you don't want to do.

We believe that it's unnecessary to use trance or other techniques that involve you losing control. In fact, we would go so far as to say that until you're strong enough in your basic skills to prevent a trance situation from occurring, you shouldn't be working with Spirit. There are plenty of very good, experienced

Mediums who don't need to use such techniques in order to work. It's important to remember that any communication has to be two-way, and if someone is talking to you and you're in trance, and therefore not listening, then you aren't communicating. If you feel that a spirit is attempting to talk through you and you don't like it, you can simply state 'No' very firmly and they won't be able to 'use' you in this way.

If you're working in a group you should never feel forced into doing anything that makes you feel uncomfortable or fearful. This is dangerous. You should always feel in control.

Being able to communicate well with your Guides is essential as they provide a barrier between you and the other side. Inform them of your boundaries as you work and learn to develop your skills while in full control. Start with developing good basic skills, opening, protection and closing. (See Appendix E for methods of protection). Also ensure that those you work with know your boundaries and are confident in ensuring that they can bring you back to a fully aware state of consciousness if required. If you feel at all uneasy or as though your control is slipping, then get yourself back to full consciousness and, if necessary out of the situation or area of influence of any negative entity that may be causing the problem.

If you wish to develop into trance work at a later stage that's fine, but it isn't essential. Spirit possession is, thankfully, very rare and as long as you work with the right intentions and remember to protect yourself you should be fine.

Doesn't this type of work drain your energy?

Any kind of work can have a physical or mental intensity that can be tiring and people often mistake this for becoming psychically drained. However, we believe that it shouldn't be a drain of your own spiritual energy if you do it properly. It's essential that you learn the basics of energy work – working with auras and chakras, protection and grounding. Also, build up slowly and if you feel your energy start to dip, take a break. Spirit do use our auric energy to communicate and manifest and you can feel tired. If you can learn to 'plug in' to universal energy you shouldn't feel drained. We find that after running a workshop or working intensely in a psychic way we're buzzing with energy – and often very hungry! However, after between 30 and 60 minutes our energy levels crash. But then it's often late at night anyway, and we do sleep very well afterwards! This is more down to energy fluctuations. When you work, you learn to build up the energy in the room with exercises and visualisations, sometimes even chanting and drumming. We experience a high level of energy in the room that's used by Spirit to do their work, then we experience the lack of energy that follows, but it's not our own life force being drained and is therefore not detrimental in any way, if done correctly. Understanding Psychic Protection is essential, read the questions on it in this book for more information (see also Appendix E).

How do I know who to work psychically with?

Use your intuition. Work with people that you instantly feel comfortable with and who want to work in the same way as you. We always work in love and light and state this at the start of all our groups and workshops. If someone thought this was odd or refused to work with this intention we would not work with them. We've both worked with many different wonderful people but you sometimes come across people that you feel uncomfortable with. You must trust your gut feeling. We tend to find that the universe finds its own level with this and those who have come to our groups or workshops that haven't been right for us haven't returned for whatever reason. We were obviously not right for them either. But when you find the right people they can become very dear friends, almost family. We hope that you're all as lucky as we've been in this respect.

When I meditate, sense a spirit or do readings, I get tears in my eyes but I'm not crying. What's that all about?

This is quite a common reaction to being sensitive to a spirit presence and happens to both of us a lot. It could be a physical way of us knowing that they're close. Another theory is that as their very different energy vibrations collide with our own, it causes some form of physical sensation or reaction, such as heat or cold, and when a very strong connection occurs the physical sensation can cause tears to form even if you aren't remotely sad. We also find that it can happen as a sign from Spirit that we're speaking the truth when discussing spiritual or philosophical matters. If this happens you should take a special note of where you are, any other feelings, sensations or thoughts that you're having at the time, or what you're discussing.

People talk about psychic protection, what is this?

Psychic protection is anything that strengthens your aura and creates a safe place around you that nothing negative can penetrate.

There are a number of reasons for requiring psychic protection:
- Leaky auras - if it's yours, you'll become drained of energy, or if it's someone else's they can pass on their negativities.
- In the presence of 'auric vampires'. This is the term given to those who, often subconsciously, take your energy.
- In times of vulnerability such as during meditation, when working with Spirit or when you're low.
- In rare cases of psychic attack, or if someone is being angry, resentful or negative towards you.
- If you suspect you're empathic, or sensitive to the emotions of others.

From our experiences it's essential to protect yourself before undertaking any form of spiritual or psychic work, including meditation or healing. In all our combined years of working we haven't encountered 'evil' spirits or bad energies that have impacted on us. We firmly believe that this is because we've always been extremely vigilant about working in a safe and protected manner. We've also ensured that we've been working in ways and with people we feel safe with and that we remained observant of energy changes so that we could take steps to remain in a positive atmosphere. If you take only one piece of advice from this book, please take this: ALWAYS PROTECT YOURSELF WHEN YOU WORK.

How do I protect myself?

There are many ways of protecting yourself some of which are listed below. Try them out and choose the one that you feel most comfortable and confident with.

- Visualisation: Imagine some form of protective shield around you and your aura. This could be a force field of bright white light, a bubble, an egg, mirrors reflecting away from you or see yourself being inside a hollow crystal filled with light. Know that you're safe, completely sealed in and protected from outside influences.

- Talisman: Wearing a crystal or symbol can act as protection. Look into it in detail and find something appropriate and comfortable for you. For some it could be a religious symbol, or an item given to them by a loved one. The best crystal we have found for protection is Black Tourmaline.
- Physical: Crossing your ankles and wrists seals your energy circuit not allowing others to tap into it. In some cases, you probably do this automatically.
- Ask: Before beginning any psychic or spiritual development work or if you ever feel uneasy or the need for some Psychic Protection, ask your Spirit Guides, Angels or loved ones in Spirit to draw close to you and keep you safe and protected.
- Grounding: After any psychic or spiritual development work it's essential to ground your energies to prevent you from remaining too open and picking up on everything around you. (See Appendix D for a Grounding Visualisation).
- Ongoing maintenance: Keep your own energy levels up, keep healthy and positive, have or give yourself healing or Reiki regularly, take exercise, work on strengthening your aura and practice visualisations, take time to rest and enjoy yourself.

All this will help to ensure that you're working at optimum and are able to deal with any situations that may require protection. Also, be aware of your own negative thoughts and actions and the effects they could have on yourself and others.

SPOOKY STUFF

I see coloured balls of light or sparkles, and have photographed orbs. What are they?

We believe that orbs are spirits in energy form. They're sometimes visible to the naked eye, especially to people who have developed their psychic abilities. They often show on digital photographs too – look out for small spheres, sometimes with intricate patterns within them. Why not ask for an orb to be present as you take a picture and see what happens. During ghost hunting investigations, photographs and video film are taken where temperature or electro-magnetic frequencies fluctuate, as it's common for orbs to appear on images taken in these locations. However, dust and other physical phenomena should be discounted as much as possible.

Sometimes you may see a little flurry of tiny sparkles as though a tub of glitter has been sprinkled in the air, which usually only lasts a few seconds. This can also be a spirit presence but is easier to see with the naked eye than orbs. We don't know why we see orbs or sparkles, it's probably Spirit's way of manifesting and letting us know they're around.

A word of caution, if you get bright flashes of light at the edge of your vision combined with floaters in your eye this could be caused by a medical condition and medical attention should be sought immediately. If you're in any doubt, get it checked out.

Sometimes when I look in the mirror my face seems different. Why is this?

This is a far more common phenomenon than people realise, it just doesn't really get talked about much! We both experienced this at a very young age and it can feel very frightening if you don't understand why it's happening. We believe that when it appears as though your face has changed in your reflection, it's simply a physical manifestation of a spirit presence. It's important to remember that they don't mean you any harm when they make themselves known to you in this way, even if you feel uncomfortable when it happens. Understanding protective measures (see Appendix E) and engaging with your Guides can prevent this continuing to happen should you not wish it to. Despite our initial experiences and concerns, we later came to realise that Spirit are very adept at using this technique to establish communication with us and provide us with visual proof of their existence beyond the physical. It's often known as 'overshadowing' and can progress to trance mediumship should you wish. If you do wish to work in this way, please ensure that you protect yourself and only work with experienced people that you trust.

I see things out of the corner of my eye but when I look again they're gone. Am I imagining it?

It's possible that you're imagining it or that your mind is making more out of a simple shape, shadow or movement. However, it's also possible that what you're seeing, however fleetingly, is the movement of a more subtle, or spirit, energy. People often see spirits in this way. Always look for a physical reason first, and if there doesn't appear to be one, it may be that you either have a lot of spirit activity around you at this moment in time, or that you've a natural ability to see Spirit. Are there other things going on around you that could indicate this? Has someone close to you passed recently? You may want to develop your skills to enhance them and 'see' more. As you do so, you'll see them more within your field of vision rather than on the periphery.

I do believe in this kind of thing but I've never seen a ghost. Why not?

Despite lots of ghost stories perpetually doing the rounds, seeing ghosts isn't a common experience for most people. More common are strange, seemingly un-explained phenomena or having a weird feeling in certain locations.

So, do you want to see a ghost? Maybe you just haven't been in the right place at the right time. If you wish to experience supernatural sightings why not go on some ghosts tours or visit allegedly haunted locations and see what you experience. Al-ternatively, develop your skills on courses and workshops and research the subject for yourself. You'll be surprised at what you'll learn and start to see and feel. If you only wish to do so to satisfy your curiosity, to have a story to tell or offer proof that they exist, we would suggest that the chances are that you won't ever see one. Some-times you have to have faith first. This opens your mind ready to receive.

Many people can't actually see Spirit physically manifest, including top Mediums and plenty of people go their whole lives without seeing a ghost. When working with Spirit we receive information in a number of ways, by seeing – clairvoyance, hearing – clairaudience or by sensations or feelings – clairsentience. One or two of these methods will usually be more prominent for you. Everyone is different, so you may be more gifted at hearing or sensing than seeing Spirit. In time, as you develop your skills, you may find that your ability to see Spirit improves.

We seem to get a lot of electrical disturbances at home. Someone said we could have a ghost, is this true?

You could, although it would be worth getting the wiring checked first! Seriously, if it's not the wiring it could be Spirit trying to get your attention. They 'pull' on various forms of energy in order to manifest or to make things happen. And they seem to find it easy, and fun, to make lights turn on or off, flicker or even to cause bulbs to blow. Don't panic, they're most probably being friendly. Ask yourself, are you ignoring them? Are you ignoring your calling to work psychically? Has someone you know passed recently? They could just be saying they're okay. Acknowledge them and thank them for letting you know and ask that they move on happily and stop messing with the electrics. Do you suspect that you may have a more complex situ-ation or a haunting? If so, read on for our other questions on this subject.

I sometimes feel like someone is watching me or that I'm not alone. Do you know what it could be?

Most probably you'll be sensing the energy of a loved one in Spirit watching over you and just letting you know that they're around. Occasionally it could be a spirit presence unrelated to you, perhaps associated with the property you're in when you experience it. As long as it doesn't make you feel uncomfortable, don't worry. Acknowledge them and ask them to move on.

This also suggests that you may be clairsentient (sensing Spirit) and you may wish to consider developing this ability further.

I sometimes feel like someone is watching me or that I'm not alone. It feels weird. What should I do?

If these feelings make you feel uncomfortable or frightened in any way there a number of techniques you can try, if you wish, before calling in a Medium or similar. Firstly, learn the principles of psychic protection. Ask your Spirit Guides and Angels to come forward and help you by offering their protection and to encourage the presence to leave. Then ask the presence to leave. Out loud is best. Simply say, without sounding angry or antagonistic, "Please leave you're making me feel uneasy". This should do the trick, however, if, after this, you feel it's necessary, you should seek help from an experienced Medium, or a Rescue Circle from a Spiritualist Church or similar. A Rescue Circle specialises in getting rid of problem spirits.

You may wish to read the questions regarding 'Protection' on page 55 of this book (see also Appendix E).

Why do you get cold spots or draughts when spirits are around?

There are several theories on this, but as with most of these issues we can't say that we know for sure. It should also be noted that some people experience a rise in temperature when Spirit are around and our answers relate to this phenomenon too.

Helen says: When Spirit attempt to get our attention or make their presence known, by manifestation or moving objects, they require a lot of energy.

The physical world isn't their realm, it's too dense so they need to utilise energy from living beings. They do this by pulling energy from the auras of those nearby. This energy movement feels to us like a draught or cold spot.

Diane says: Two theories seem most likely to me. Firstly, that it's a way of Spirit grabbing our attention. And secondly, that they exist on a different energy vibration which we sense or feel as hot or cold when it comes into contact with our auras.

I keep hearing someone calling my name. What's going on?

This is a very common occurrence. We believe it's a spirit, often your Guide trying to get your attention. It can be an indication that you've a natural gift for clairaudiency (psychic hearing). If you want to stop 'hearing', you can employ basic psychic protection techniques (see Appendix E). Or, if you want to develop this skill you can try answering 'yes' to the 'voice' and see if you establish a line of communication. You could also seek to develop your skills by starting with meditation and other workshops or joining a development circle, perhaps at a Spiritualist Church.

What's it like to see a ghost?

Helen says: Actually physically seeing one? To be honest, a lot of the time you don't even realise that you've seen one until afterwards. There have been occasions when I've seen them and stood looking, saying quite calmly, yet quizzically to myself, 'Is that what I think it is?' Other times they make you jump and you say something out loud which usually makes the spirit disappear in surprise! I think this is because it takes a lot of energy for them to manifest (show themselves) and they seem to be easily startled which must make them lose concentration and vanish. I tell people not to worry about it too much though as actual physical sightings aren't so common. If you're seeing out of the ordinary stuff, perhaps in your own home, then you should look into it further and read some of our other FAQ's on this subject as well as those on protection.

What's really odd though is when one goes through you. That's not so much scary as weird. It can feel cold, it can make you dizzy or a little nauseous, it can be a sort of shudder (you know the phrase 'a ghost just walked over my grave'?)

and you may feel as though you need to almost shake the feeling off afterwards. Although, if they brush past you they can feel as though they're much more solid and real. It's a strange sensation that's very hard to describe.

Diane says: It's unusual to actually see a 'fully-formed' ghost in front of you, it's far more common to see shadows or glimpses of things out of the corner of your eye. Despite doing this work for many years, I still feel surprised when I see one in it's entirety, and as Helen says that surprise often makes them disappear. I'm confident with the protection that I always have around me though and so I never fear ghosts that I sense or see.

Why do animals and children sense or see spirits when we don't?

It's true that animals and children see and sense Spirit more easily than adults. We believe that children are much more aware of Spirit because they haven't been conditioned not to believe. They have no limiting beliefs of what's 'normal' compared with those of us who have been in the physical world for a longer period of time and who may have bought into the more human concepts and beliefs of what should and shouldn't happen. As we get older we become more used to seeing the more dense energy of physical things and start to filter out the more subtle energies of the Spirit Realms . That is unless we deliberately choose not to by actively developing the spiritual and psychic side of ourselves, or because it's so strong within us that we can't filter it out.

Animals seem to sense subtle energies and changes in energy that humans generally don't. It's well documented that many animals react in the moments before an earthquake or other natural event where humans have no idea that anything is brewing. There are also many stories of animals 'knowing' that their owners are in trouble and going to their aid. Again, they don't have anyone sitting saying to them, 'Oh you're imagining that, it's all in your head' etc. as many young people do, so animals maintain their awareness of the non-physical throughout their time on this earth.

My kids talk to people who aren't there. Do you think we might have a ghost?

It's possible. Kids do have very active imaginations, however they're also more sensitive and accepting of spirit presences. If your child has an imaginary friend it could be that it's more than an active imagination. Often they are spirit children who just want to play, or it could be their Spirit Guide, or a passed relative who is looking out for them. You could try to ask some simple questions to find out information about the 'person' that may be able to be substantiated. Watch out for other signs of paranormal activity, and if appropriate, teach your child about basic protection. If they're too young for this, buy them a protection crystal or amulet just in case. Look out for stress or anxiety, without worrying the child of course, and if you become concerned over activity or their behaviour, seek assistance from an experienced Medium, healer or Rescue Circle. They should be able to assist with a healing on your property and not even involve your child. In fact, it would be best if any healing work could be done while the kids are out. But don't be surprised if they somehow know that things are different afterwards.

Things keep going missing at home and then turning up in strange places or somewhere I've already looked. What's going on?

This is so common and frequently put down to forgetfulness, absent-mindedness or our busy lifestyles. We think that it's spirits having a bit of fun, getting our attention and letting us know they're around. Are the objects special? Or linked to someone who has passed? Does it occur around an anniversary or has someone passed fairly recently? The spirits of young children are especially keen on making themselves known in this way. You can have strong words with them and tell them to stop it. This often works. Equally, if the items haven't turned up again, try asking out loud that they be returned. The items usually turn up again very quickly.

If the objects are ones which, when missing, slow you down, such as a wallet, keys or something else that you never leave the house without, it could be someone in Spirit protecting you. We often hear of, and have personally experienced, situations where one is slowed down and misses potentially being involved in an accident. If this happens to you, thank your 'Angels' for looking out for you.

Additionally you can call on your Guides, Angels or loved ones in Spirit to assist in finding genuinely lost items. The item often turns up in a really obvious place soon after. Or you suddenly remember or are drawn to where it is.

What causes ghosts and hauntings?

There are three types of haunting:

- Residual – this is like a psychic imprint or recording of an event that has been left on a location or object. It would be similar to someone projecting a film on to a screen. This is why there are often reports of a 'replay' of historic events on certain dates. Now, clearly, while this may be a bit odd at first, it's not going to cause you any threat of harm.
- Visitation – a spirit often visits certain people or locations, possibly out of curiosity or to pass on a message. They're spirits who seem to be able to pass easily between different realms of existence.
- Earthbound – a spirit that didn't pass over to the Spiritual Realm when their physical body died and remain 'stuck' here until they're shown how to cross over.

We've got a ghost at home... but they're quite friendly. Shall we just leave them alone?

You can if you wish, as long as they aren't causing any problem, or giving an indication of being tormented or trapped here. It should always be remembered however, that this is no longer their world and they shouldn't really be present on the physical plane. Diane once heard it said that ghosts aren't pets. You can't just keep them in your home because you like them! We think that's a fair point.

We believe that earthbound spirits should be helped to 'go into the light' rather than remain here after their time. However don't confuse these spirits with transient visits from loved ones from the other side who are happily 'in the light' and can pop over now and again for a visit.

We've got a ghost at home... and we don't like it. What can we do?

Contact a very good Medium or healer who is experienced in such matters, or a 'Rescue Circle' who specialise in getting rid of problem spirits. Your local Spiritualist Church will be able to point you in the right direction. An experienced Medium will be able to help your unwanted guest to 'go into the light' and leave you in peace. Some may charge for this, others may ask for a donation. It's better to get a recommended and experienced person involved than attempt to sort it out yourself. Ensure that you're comfortable with the person you've called in and with their methods. Talk through what they plan to do before you decide to proceed. You may wish to read the questions regarding 'Protection' in this book (see also Appendix E).

What are poltergeists and are they dangerous?

'Poltergeist' means 'noisy spirit'. They're earthbound spirits who refuse to believe that they're dead and subsequently become frustrated and maybe even angry. This frustration and anger can manifest in disruptive behaviour, strange noises, with or without any obvious cause, and they can sometimes move objects. This can become unpleasant and disturbing to those living with one. They can be dangerous, but it's rare. They're usually connected to a house rather than a person.

If you, or someone you know experiences unexplained activity like this and thinks that they have a poltergeist, professional and experienced Mediums and healers should be called upon. Contact a recommended Medium or your local Spiritualist Church. They'll be able to find you what's known as a 'Rescue Circle' who specialise in this type of problem. As mentioned before, ensure that you're comfortable with the person you've called in, and with their methods.

We sometimes hear unexplained noises in our house or workplace, could we have a poltergeist?

It's quite possible, although a physical explanation should always be sought first. General noises tend to have a rational explanation such as creaky floorboards, old pipes etc. Helen thought she may have had a poltergeist visiting once but discovered it was a minor earthquake that had rattled the roof tiles! (It did take her by surprise and wake her up in the middle of the night.)

You may wish to find out about the history of the property and previous owners and see if there could be any reason for the activity. You could also ask a Medium or local psychic circle to visit the location, without telling them anything, and see what they come up with. It could be a very harmless spirit visitor who is just being noisy and it'll be sufficient to simply have stern words with them and ask that they leave you in peace.

Is there anything in the old parlour games like table tipping, automatic writing or seances?

Yes, there can be. There are many different forms of psychic work and these are an example of some. They can be used as any other tool in communicating with Spirit, but they have to be given the respect they deserve. See the following question on Ouija Boards but basically only do them if you're very experienced, with people you really trust and connect with, who work in a positive way, and always use protection!

I've been told never to do a Ouija Board as I might get possessed. Can this happen and is it really dangerous?

Ok, Answer 1 – Yes, it can be dangerous and we would strongly discourage anyone who is inexperienced in psychic work to use a Ouija Board. In fact, you should be *very* experienced before undertaking anything like this. We would particularly discourage teenagers from having a go, especially for fun. A reason for this is that, typically, the energy associated with 'doing a Ouija Board' tends to be one of fear. Negative entities can use this to manifest physical activity and audio/visual phenomena. This causes more fear and therefore a negative cycle can begin, feeding the entity and possibly resulting in a spirit attachment – or possession. Additionally we know that earthbound spirits find it easy to communicate via Ouija Boards. While these types of spirit aren't all problematic, if you *are* unfortunate to have a bad experience, it will be with an earthbound and if you can't deal with it due to your lack of experience and growing fear it'll simply become worse and scarier.

Answer 2 – Please read answer 1 first! They don't have to be dangerous. They can be excellent tools for Spirit communication if all of those taking part:

- have a very good foundation in psychic practices.
- are confident in protection, connecting and communicating with their own Spirit Guide, sensing energy and closing down.
- work regularly together and trust one another 100%.
- aren't fearful of Spirit communication or of the board.
- have a positive outlook and only work with the most positive of intentions.
- don't use a permanent board. Make one from paper and destroy it after use.
- aren't suffering from any form of mental illness, spiritual crisis or similar problems and have no history of it.

Do *not* use a Ouija Board if you're not 100% confident and comfortable. Be sure to find out how to do it properly first, and ensure that you protect yourself extremely well before you begin. Really, we would suggest that you're far better to use an alternative method to connect with the Spirit World. (See also the questions on psychic protection and Appendix E).

How can horoscopes be correct if each sign applies to one twelfth of the population?

Horoscopes that are written for papers and magazines focus on just one small element of your astrological make up. This is known as the Sun Sign and relates to the position of the sun on the day that you were born. However, a more detailed examination of your full astrological birth chart, showing the position of all the planets, and the moon, and their relationships to each other at the time of your birth provides a much more accurate description of your characteristics. Astrology used in this more specific way can be used to predict trends likely to affect or influence you. While Sun sign predictions can appear to be accurate for some, they're by no means the full extent of what astrology can do for you.

So, what do you think of U.F.O.'s?

Our thoughts on this are that U.F.O.'S can usually be explained by something quite rational. They could be military craft that are being tested. Or they may well be visitors from other worlds or from other dimensions, or be highly evolved beings from Spirit. Reports of U.F.O.'s certainly aren't a new thing, there are cave paintings dating back hundreds of years depicting these types of encounters. And it would be quite arrogant of us to assume we're the only living creatures in the vastness of space, even more so that we're the most intelligent!

What do you think creates crop circles?

We're still undecided on this subject. There are a few theories on crop circles, ranging from geological or meteorological anomalies, UFO's, experimental but nonetheless man-made aircraft and equipment, to people. Earliest recordings of crop circles are found in the 1600's in England, more recently they increased in number between 1970 and 2000. A study in 2000 found evidence proving that 80% of crop circles were manmade. Sadly some people insist that crop circles have a paranormal cause even in the face of individuals coming forward and saying 'it was us and this is how we did it'. A desire for the existence of, and proof for, something more than the physical should always be weighed up with the rational possibilities before a conclusion is drawn. However, one must ask, if 80% are definitely manmade, what did cause the other 20%?

There's no proof for any of this stuff. Isn't it all a load of mumbo jumbo?

There may not currently be scientific evidence for lots of esoteric beliefs and paranormal encounters, but new findings in quantum physics are providing some theories and evidence. And simply because we don't have proof, does it make it any less real for those who experience this kind of thing? After all perceived threat is no less fear inducing than an actual threat. And, very often, today's science would have been yesterday's magic. Maybe those challenging us to prove our theories should be challenged to disprove them instead? This, after all, is what scientists have to do with their hypotheses. We like the following quote. We believe it to be true in most cases and explains why we, personally, never seek to prove ourselves to others.

"For those who believe, no proof is necessary.
For those who don't believe, no proof is possible."
Stuart Chase

Do magic and spells really work?

In our experience they most definitely do. You should read our questions on healing (p.25), cosmic ordering (p.33) and psychic attack and curses (below) along with this answer, as they're very similar. Magic and spells can work, as can healing and prayer. We believe that when you cast a spell you're harnessing your ability to manifest in a very focussed, and thus powerful, way. However, if you're going down that route you should be aware that what you give out, you get back. That goes for good as well as ill. Work of this nature should only be done in love and light, for the higher good of all and never to cause harm, upset or to manipulate anyone. If you have a specific interest in spellcraft, paganism, witchcraft or Wicca you should research it further and remember the Witch's creed, 'Harm None'.

Are you a witch then?

Helen says: Well that depends entirely on your definition of a witch. I don't like labels but lots of people I know, and many of their children, will affectionately call me one. Personally, I work with Spirit, in love and light always, and with the highest intentions. I try to stay in harmony with the universe, with nature's rhythms and with my true self. I'm happy with that, does it matter what label it gives me? If you want to know about the many varied definitions of the word 'witch' do some research on the subject. You may well be surprised at what you discover.

Diane says: I prefer not to label myself as anything. My beliefs are a unique, in-dividual set of beliefs, my own truth. Not that I have anything against witches – I have met some perfectly lovely white witches in my time! As long as they work for a higher good that's fine with me.

Are there such things as psychic attacks or curses?

Helen says: There can be, although, in our experience they're rare. Alot of what you experience as a result of something like this would be dependent on your belief in it. If you're aware of negative thoughts being focussed on you, do you believe that they have any power? If you do, the chances are that they will. If you don't, that will also be true! There are exceptions: in which case you should read up on psychic protection (p.55 or Appendix E) and, if necessary, seek advice from someone who can help you, perhaps at your local Spiritualist Church or a psychic healer or teacher with experience of these matters. I believe that you get back what you give out. Do you always work in love and light with the purest of intentions towards all? There's a Native American saying that I hold with, "Walk with your face to the sunlight, and you will not see the shadow".

Diane says: Every thought we have has an energy of its own and energy creates matter. Just as a positive thought can help to manifest good, lots of negative thoughts can create bad scenarios. So if a person 'curses' someone else, it can cause a problem. But it can be remedied with the help of a reputable and experienced healer or Medium. Psychic attack is usually believed to be the result of a spirit attacking a person; again, it's possible, but extremely rare. Always work with protection and in love and light to avoid such problems arising. Please read our questions on protection on page 55 or see Appendix E.

If I empty my mind will the devil jump in?

Firstly do you believe in the devil? If not, do you need to ask the question? If you do, well, have you ever actually tried to empty your mind? It's virtually impossible. Some religious individuals believe that we clear our minds during meditation, however, when we meditate we usually begin by focussing on our breathing, therefore our minds aren't empty, we're thinking about our breath. Our minds are no emptier when we're meditating than when we begin falling asleep. Does the devil jump in then? If you're concerned with spirit possession, don't be, it's extremely rare and easily avoided by taking certain precautions. Read our questions on protection on page 55 or see Appendix E.

I want a tarot reading done but I'm scared of the death card turning up. What can I do?

Don't be. Firstly, the 'death' card does not mean death in the physical sense. The Death card is always a very positive card representing the end of a cycle or the 'death' of the old, perhaps outdated attitudes or unnecessary elements of your life and the inevitable start of something new. It symbolises exciting times ahead as changes comes into your life. All Tarot Cards are symbolic and it's down to the skill of the reader to interpret and communicate the messages held within the reading to the enquirer. If you're still concerned, ring round a few readers and find one that uses cards other than the traditional Tarot. Try an 'Angel Card' reading or another alternative.

Can people really have out of body experiences?

Yes, we believe so. The technique is also known as 'Astral Projection'. A part of our being, the 'astral body' is said to temporarily separate from the physical body and 'travel' through distance, time or space to observe other events, or possibly take messages to individuals. This is a skill that can be learnt but it can also happen spontaneously while asleep. People who undergo extreme ordeals such as abuse or torture often report being able to 'step outside' of their body and remain detached from the scenario. There are reports from people in surgery or who have been clinically dead that they got up and looked back at themselves being treated. They've even been able to tell the medical staff what they were saying and doing at the time. It's even possible for people in comas to leave their physical bodies and visit their loved ones.

It's perfectly safe to astral travel as our 'astral body' is connected to our physical body by the 'astral cord'. Some people describe this as a thick, silver, umbilical-like cord that's only broken at the moment of our physical death.

A similar technique known as 'remote viewing' is when a person can psychically view a different location in time and space working through the 3rd eye chakra. It's suggested by some that government agencies have experimented with remote viewing in order to obtain vital or highly sensitive information from others.

What about near death experiences?

Having worked with Spirit for so long we completely believe in these. We've had many experiences of connecting with the Spirit World and have no hesitation in saying that we can travel between the physical and Spiritual Realms. Near death experiences are best described as a different type of 'out of body experience' that occurs at the time of imminent death or danger from which the person subsequently survives.

These episodes often have similar themes. For example, travelling along a tunnel, seeing a bright light at the end and possibly seeing loved ones or Angels ready to greet them. This is often accompanied by feelings of love and serenity that transcend any earthly experiences. The experience usually ends when either thoughts of their loved ones 'back home' or feelings of unfinished business enter their consciousness, or they hear a voice that tells them to return to their physical body.

Anecdotal evidence suggests that when such an extreme event happens to someone, they subsequently view things very differently, especially if they've not previously considered the spiritual aspect of life, and death. They make changes, appreciate life more fully and live differently because they have a realisation that there's more to life than what's in the material here and now. Encouragingly, most no longer have any fear of dying.

Isn't all of this frightening?

Mostly no. It's usually the anticipation in our minds that's scarier than actually experiencing something paranormal. A lack of understanding can also contribute to fear of any such phenomena.

This may be controversial, but contrary to popular, media-led, opinion paranormal encounters aren't usually that scary. As we get older our brains get bombarded with Hollywood imagery and fuelled by teenage urban myths, which cause our minds to associate Spirit activity with something really scary and dangerous. As a result, a lot of us put barriers up which can stunt our personal, spiritual and psychic development. In the majority of cases, when an event is encountered it's usually met with a sense of acceptance.

Helen says: "As a child, when I saw a spirit walking through our family home, I just asked my Mum, "Who's that lady?' Although, to be fair, waking up to see a spirit standing in your home in the middle of the night was not always so pleasant as both my sisters will also attest to."

We hope that by reading frank, sensible books such as this one, some element of this fear will be reduced for you, so that you may be able to experience the positive uplifting side of these experiences instead. On the practical side, if you wish to take the psychic aspect further, familiarising yourself with and using protective measures is essential (see Appendix E). Remember this is our realm, not theirs and we are in control. Good development groups and practice will help you to control any communication with Spirit and with understanding and knowledge you'll feel less frightened. You'd be pretty scared if you went scuba diving without knowing how to make your air and equipment work properly wouldn't you? Psychic abilities are the same as any other skill in this respect.

APPENDIX A
PSYCHOMETRY EXERCISE

Get a group together and each bring along a personal item, such as a piece of jewellery. Have each person place their item in a bag or bowl with a cloth over it as they arrive, without allowing others to see it. The bag or bowl should be taken round to each person in turn, who, without looking should take one item, ensuring that it's not their own.

Hold the item in your hands, closing your eyes if necessary. Breathing slowly and deeply, relax you body and allow your mind to clear as you attempt to tune into the energy of the object. Shut out everything else, focussing only on this single item. Feel its weight, its texture its temperature. What else do you notice?

Allow images to form in your mind's eye, take note of fragrances, feelings, sensations, words that pop into your head, sounds that you hear. What are you doing with the object? How are you handling it? That can also mean something to or represent something about the owner. For example, twisting and turning an object in your hands could indicate that the person is restless, or feels that they're going round in circles with a problem. Or it may have been a familiar action of a particular loved one.

Sit quietly for a few minutes and write down anything that comes to you. Don't try to analyse it, just put down anything that you get. After a while some of you may feel that you know whose item you're holding. Let each person guess at whose object they have in their hands, but don't worry if you aren't correct, it takes practice.

Take time for each person to feed back the information that they've received to the person whose item they've read. Continue to hold the item as you do this as more may come to you as you talk and get feedback. Swap around until everyone has given their messages.

Practice this exercise lots. It's a great starting point for developing your psychic abilities and it's fun. Some may find they have a natural ability, but others may not get anything at all on their first attempt.

APPENDIX B
MEDITATION EXERCISE

Take your attention to each area of your body in turn, starting with your feet and working upwards, including your face and head. Tense and hold each muscle group for a few seconds and then consciously release them. Take your time and don't rush through. You may want to repeat this exercise a second time.

Then take your awareness to your breathing, preferably through your nose, as this is more relaxing. Take a slow, deep breath in for a count of four if you can, hold the breath for two and then exhale slowly for a count of four. Continue in this way, focusing on the breath and counting. If your mind drifts or you lose track, start counting again and refocus on your breathing. It's not a race or a competition, just a way of relaxing and focusing your mind on the moment. You can start to lengthen the breath once you're used to it, increasing the inhalation and exhalation to 5 or 6 counts, take your time though.

Start by meditating for just 5 minutes at a time, preferably at the same time every day. Gradually increase the time until you're meditating for around 20 minutes at a time, by then, you'll have it.

BASIC COLOUR INFORMATION

Red: If you surround yourself with, love the colour or have lots of red in your aura you are: Passionate, active, courageous and strong with lots of vitality.
Caution: Too much exposure can cause anger, impulsiveness and hunger.
Use red to add some 'get up and go' to your life.

Orange: If you surround yourself with, love the colour or have lots of orange in your aura you are: Joyful and happy, an optimistic, independent and social person.
Caution: Too much can cause restlessness.
Use orange to cheer yourself up and give you confidence.

Yellow: If you surround yourself with, love the colour or have lots of yellow in your aura you are: Intellectual, creative and artistic, an open and articulate person.
Caution: Over exposure can cause over-thinking and over-analysing. It can also make you too open to the influences of others.
Use yellow to awaken clairsentient abilities and to bring happiness into your life.

Green: If you surround yourself with, love the colour or have lots of green in your aura you are: affectionate, loyal and trustworthy. You are full of sympathy and compassion and strive for health and harmony.
Caution: Don't let others walk all over you.
Use green to promote calm, relaxation, healing and balance.

Pink: If you surround yourself with, love the colour or have lots of pink in your aura you are: Charming and delicate, a peacemaker, full of love and compassion.
Caution: Over exposure can lead to indecisiveness, immaturity and lack of focus.
Use pink to attract love, protection and security and to learn to appreciate the finer things in life.

More overleaf >>

Blue: If you surround yourself with, love the colour or have lots of blue in your aura you are: Good at communication, listening skills and self-expression. You're serious and cautious. Blue is linked with clairaudience.
Caution: Too much can be linked to someone who's over cautious, a worrier and is oversensitive.
Use blue to attract tranquillity, and to learn to communicate your concerns.

Purple: If you surround yourself with, love the colour or have lots of purple in your aura you are: Strong, sensitive, spiritual and intuitive. It's linked with Clairvoyance and ESP. You're a visionary and are passionate about your beliefs.
Caution: Over exposure can cause you to be overbearing, feel misunderstood and become aloof.
Use purple to develop your spiritual and psychic side.

White: If you surround yourself with, love the colour or have lots of white in your aura you are: A very spiritual person, an idealist and an innovator. You may seem shy but you do voice your opinions. You're seeking and are aware of the process of enlightenment.
Caution: Don't think of yourself as more important than others.
Use white to help simplify your life, seek the truth and awaken greater creativity.

Black: It is highly unusual to have black in your aura and usually means it needs a bit of healing, extra protection and energising.
If you surround yourself with or love the colour black you are: Seeking knowledge, intense, introspective and have hidden depths.
Caution: You may be trying to hide in the shadows or be suppressing your desires.
Use black to look within.

APPENDIX D

GROUNDING VISUALISATION

This exercise takes you through the basics of 'grounding' your energy. It should be done following any type of spiritual or psychic development work, including meditation, or even if you have just been having a philosophical conversation and feel a bit 'spaced out'. Read it through to familiarise yourself with it and then work through the instructions slowly, one by one. It is written in such a way that you could also read it aloud to others if you were doing some meditation or other work in a group.

Sit in a comfortable position and close your eyes.

Bring your attention to your breathing and focus on it for a few breaths.

Take your awareness to the invisible energy field surrounding you and visualise it drawing in close around your physical body.

Take your awareness to the area just above your crown and see a small sphere of light sitting here.

Imagine that sphere of light shrinking in size and sinking down through the crown of your head.

See it slowly descending down past the brow.

Into the throat.

Then following the line of the spine, down, through your body, towards your heart area.

Down to your solar plexus.

Through the abdominal area.

To the base of your spine.

Now visualise the sphere of energy either leaving through the base of your spine, or dividing in two and sinking down through the your legs and leaving through the soles of your feet.

Feel this energy leaving you and connecting with the earth. Visualise roots extending out and down deep into the earth.

Become more aware of your feet and your physical body.

More overleaf >>

Let us take a moment to thank our Spirit Guides, Angels and loved ones in Spirit for their presence, protection and wisdom while we've been working. Know that they will always be on hand should we need to call on them.

Now bring your awareness back to your physical body, the chair you're sitting on, your contact with the floor.

Begin to bring some movement back into your fingers and toes.

In your own time opening your eyes, you are fully awake and aware and in the physical world.

If you're working in a group and reading this aloud ensure that at this point you watch for them starting to wriggle fingers and toes and keep an eye on anyone who doesn't do this. If a member of the group appears to not want to come back to the room, simply repeat the last paragraph (in bold) but raising your voice so that it's said slightly louder and firmer. Repeat a third time if necessary, moving over to the person and at the end just saying their name quietly, placing your hand gently on their shoulder and asking that they come back now into the room.

Walking around for a little while, stamping your feet or jumping up and down helps to bring you back to the physical world.

You can also ground your energy very readily by eating a small amount of food such as a biscuit, toast or chocolate. This brings your attention to more physical demands and closes down your connection with the more subtle elements.

APPENDIX E
PROTECTION

There are many ways of protecting yourself some of which are listed below. Try them out and choose the one that you feel most comfortable and confident with.

- Visualisation: Imagine some form of protective shield around you and your aura. This could be a force field of bright white light, a bubble, an egg, mirrors reflecting away from you or see yourself being inside a hollow crystal filled with light. Know that you're safe, completely sealed in and protected from outside influences.
- Talisman: Wearing a crystal or symbol can act as protection. Look into it in detail and find something appropriate and comfortable for you. For some it could be a religious symbol, or an item given to them by a loved one. The best crystal we have found for protection is Black Tourmaline.
- Physical: Crossing your ankles and wrists seals your energy circuit not allowing others to tap into it. In some cases, you probably do this automatically.
- Ask: Before beginning any psychic or spiritual development work or if you ever feel uneasy or the need for some psychic protection, ask your Spirit Guides, Angels or loved ones in Spirit to draw close to you and keep you safe and protected.
- Grounding: After any psychic or spiritual development work it's essential to ground your energies to prevent you from remaining too open and picking up on everything around you. (See Appendix D for a Grounding Visualisation).
- Ongoing Maintenance: Keep your own energy levels up, keep healthy and positive, have or give yourself healing or Reiki regularly, take exercise, work on strengthening your aura and practice visualisations, take time to rest and enjoy yourself.

All of this will help to ensure that you're working at optimum and are able to deal with any situations that may require protection. Also, be aware of your own negative thoughts and actions and the effects they could have on yourself and others.

GLOSSARY OF TERMS

Please bear in mind that these are our explanations of these terms, there may be different definitions.

3RD EYE: The brow chakra is located between and slightly above our eyes. This chakra is used for and related to psychic work and remote viewing.

ADVANCED/HIGHLY EVOLVED BEINGS: Beings from the 'Spirit' or 'higher' realms with insight and knowledge of Universal wisdom and laws. They transcend the physical dimension as well as time and space.

ANGEL CARDS: Used in a similar way to Tarot but with pictures depicting different types of Angels. Other cards are also available depicting mythical creatures and other scenarios.

CIRCLE: A group of like-minded individuals who meet regularly in order to develop their spiritual beliefs and psychic or mediumistic abilities.

DIVINATION: The practice of seeking information by paranormal means. Examples are the use of cards, tea leaves and runes.

ELECTRO-MAGNETIC FIELD: The residual energy produced by and emanating from any atomic structure. Probably caused by the constant movement of its minute parts.

EMPATHIC: Usually referring to those who understand and share the feelings of others. Within the context of psychic work, this term refers to the ability to 'feel' and, very often, experience the emotions of others. Some people aren't aware that they're empathic but find it very easy to build rapport and understand others. They also feel a strong urge, almost a responsibility to help people.

GUIDED VISUALISATION: A form of meditation whereby a very descriptive narrative of a journey or experience assists those taking part in imagining or seeing it in their mind's eye.

'INTO THE LIGHT': The term used when the spirit of a deceased person moves on into the Spirit Realm. So called as many people who have near death experiences describe moving towards a bright light.

MEDIUM: A person who is able to communicate with those in the Spirit Realm.

PARANORMAL: According to the Oxford English Dictionary, this means, "supposedly beyond the scope of normal scientific understanding".

PSYCHIC: the ability to know or have access to information through 'paranormal' means.

PSYCHOMETRY: The art of providing a psychic or mediumistic reading by tuning into the energy vibrations of an object worn or carried close to the enquirer, or their deceased loved one.

REIKI: A Japanese term meaning 'Universal Life Force Energy' which has come to describe a particular 'school' or method of healing.

RESCUE: A spiritual and psychic practice for helping earthbound spirits to move on into the Spirit Realm. A 'Rescue Circle' is a group of experienced Mediums and healers who specialise in performing this work.

RUNES: A set of small tablets or stones each marked with a single letter of an ancient Germanic alphabet, used for divination purposes.

SCRYING: The practice of using a reflective surface or object, such as water, a crystal ball or dark mirror, to 'see' symbols, acquire information or to connect and communicate with Spirit.

SPIRIT: The essence, perhaps soul, of a person that continues to exist beyond the physical death of the body. Often referring to the non-physical world beyond our own where we come from before and pass on to after our life. We indicate this latter meaning by use of a capital 'S'.

SPIRITUAL: Being aware of the interconnection of everything living and of the essence or spirit that makes each of us alive and unique. Having an understanding that there's more to life than physical matter and that a part of us continues to exist after physical death.

SPIRITUALIST CHURCH: Meeting places, not normally actually churches, for Spiritualist Meetings which usually include demonstrations of mediumship, healing evenings and often workshops and development groups. Services are run along similar lines to regular churches with prayers and hymns but a Spiritualist Church is looking to provide proof of the existence of spirit after death.

SUPERNATURAL: According to the Oxford English Dictionary, "attributed to some force beyond scientific understanding of the laws of nature".

TELEPATHIC/TELEPATHY: The ability to send or receive thoughts, words or images to or from another individual by means other than the 'known' senses.

RESOURCES

WHERE TO GO FOR HELP

It's difficult for us to recommend a particular place or person without knowing them personally and having had some experience of their work. However, these are some points of contact for you that will start you off if you're in need of help. Do a bit of research in your local area, ask for recommendations and trust your intuition (UK only).

To help you find a local Spiritualist Church visit the Spiritualist National Union's website: www.snu.org

For courses, seminars and demonstrations take a look at The Arthur Findlay College in Stansted, Essex. Their website is www.arthurfindlaycollege.org

The Pagan Federation for honest and reliable information about the many types of pagan faith. www.paganfederation.org

If you have any further questions or would like to leave comments, reviews or discuss any of the subjects covered in this book, visit www.helpithinkimightbepsychic.com

**OTHER WEBSITES ASSOCIATED WITH AND PERSONALLY
RECOMMENDED BY THE AUTHORS**

www.spreadingthemagic.com
An on-line resource for personal, spiritual and psychic development. Books &
products, courses, workshops and other events and more. Plus, sign up for a
free E-newsletter.

www.stmpublishing.co.uk
For all books & products by Spreading The Magic.

www.protectedbyangels.co.uk
Find out more about healing, and put someone in the online healing book if
you feel they could benefit from help by our angels.

www.spreadingthewealth.co.uk
Exploring wealth vs. spirituality, the metaphysics of abundance and ways to
save & make money.

www.petalsinthewind.co.uk
Information on courses and workshops on psychic development held in
Hertfordshire.

www.lighting-the-way.co.uk
A website offering enlightenment and upliftment to those wishing to explore
their spiritual side.

TOP TEN RECOMMENDED READS

These are the books that have had the most impact on us and have given us the most information and inspiration over the years. We believe them to be the essential basics of anyone's library if they're looking at a more spiritual lifestyle or wishing to develop their intuitive side.

Conversations With God, Books 1, 2 & 3 *by Neale Donald Walsch*

This is a great series of books to get you thinking about spiritual philosophy.

The Secret *by Rhonda Byrne*

A fantastic read for anyone interested in creating their own reality, manifestation and the law of attraction.

Psychic Protection *by Judy Hall*

Everything you need to know about psychic protection.

Jonathan Livingstone Seagull *by Richard Bach*

For an alternative look at time and dimensions – plus anything else by this author.

The Lightworkers' Way *by Doreen Virtue*

A guide to finding your spiritual path.

Angel Numbers *by Doreen Virtue and Lynnette Brown*

If you keep getting the same individual or series of numbers cropping up in your life this little book is a brilliant tool to decipher what the Angels and the Universe are trying to tell you.

Divine Intervention *by Hazel Courtney*

One woman's journey through her own spiritual crisis.

Divine Intervention 2 Evidence for the 6th Sense *by Hazel Courtney*

The authors quest to scientifically prove many aspects of psychic and paranormal phenomena.

How to See and Read The Aura *by Ted Andrews*

Does exactly what it says. And look out for other books by this author.

Voices in My Ear *by Doris Stokes*

And anything else by this author. The book that helped us both to accept and understand the workings of Spirit.

ACKNOWLEDGEMENTS

From Helen:

Firstly, I must thank my wonderful husband John. For his love, support, honesty, wonderful creativity in designing the cover, assistance with getting the book ready, typesetting, technical wizardry and suggestions for more questions just as we were about to finish writing! He has put up with my being distracted by this project at all hours of the day and night, my excitement, my inability to sleep and my constant need to bounce ideas off him. He truly is a wonderful, calm and patient person, an angel. Oh, and I love you loads, but you already know that.

Secondly, to Diane, also an angel. Who didn't hesitate to come on board when we set out on this journey and did so with as much passion and enthusiasm as me, what more could I ask? Despite living so far apart now and so much of our collaboration having been done by text, email, rushed telephone conversations and being fitted around manic visits, work, school runs, event organising and not to mention the odd crisis, we did it girl! Thank you for your help, support, inspiration, belief, knowledge, and not to mention the laughter.

To Barry, Alicia and Louise. Thank you for loaning me your wonderful wife and mum while we've been working on this project. I hope you're as pleased with the finished work as we are. You are all stars.

I can't forget my fantastic family who gave me just the best start in all things spiritual, psychic and spooky. Mum and Dad, I bet you never knew the house was haunted when you bought it, or that your eldest daughter was quite so odd when she was born! But your influences have helped me become who I am today, thanks for letting me be me. To Paul, Julia and Fiona for putting up with me all these years and giving me the comfort that I wasn't the only one.

And a massive thanks to everyone at 'Petals', for taking me in, for always being there, and for helping me to grow into my beliefs, self belief and abilities. Keep shining the light.

To Stan, who I met in my first place of work when I was 18, you helped me answer so many questions, whether you knew it or not. You're a star. To Christina, for our long, philosophical chats late into the night whilst trying to work out the meaning and magic of life, the universe etc. Cherished times. To Marion, your workshops and crystal knowledge really set me on my path.

Everyone who I have met in my life however brief, I know that I have met for a reason. They've all been a part of my journey, and I a part of theirs, so we all take something of each other with us as we go on. Thanks to you all and I hope that I can pass a little part of my knowledge on to everyone who reads this book, and spread the magic a little more. x

From Diane:
Firstly, thanks to my amazing husband Barry, who patiently and uncomplainingly tolerates all of my many spiritual projects, most especially this book in recent months. Without your unfailing love and support I couldn't follow my true calling, and to this end, I'm forever grateful to you. I love you my darling.

To my beautiful, precious daughters, Alicia and Louise – thank you for choosing me as your mum, and for all that you teach me on a daily basis. May the Angels always bless you.

To my dear co-author, Helen, the catalyst behind this project, inspirational, but also the practical half of our duo, always willing to deal with the more mundane aspects of it all, not least the typing of our manuscript! But so much more than this, Helen has bought to my life a friendship to be treasured forever. Full of wisdom, insight, encouragement, fun, laughter and rainy days in Ludlow – I salute you and thank you my remarkable soul sister.

To Mum and Dad, the best parents a girl could ever have. And to the rest of my wonderful family, believers and sceptics among you, who encourage and support me constantly whatever your personal beliefs.

To Petals, my other family, without whom I wouldn't be the person I am today, you're more precious than you know.

To John, always so understanding of the time Helen and I have spent on this project, and always willing to unselfishly give your own time and creative skills to help with the design and formatting aspects of the book.

To all of those who have helped me on my way, the many special teachers I have been lucky enough to work with, those I have met through workshops and courses, and indeed all of my wonderful friends, thank you for touching my life with your love and generosity of spirit.

It's been an amazing journey so far, and I have no idea where else my spiritual pathway will take me, but I intend to enjoy every moment of it and I hope that this book will inspire you to do the same. As Helen says, keep spreading the magic.

From us both:

All our love and thanks go to everyone who has helped us along our way so far.

Janice, we would probably not have met each other without you. Thank you for your wisdom, support, and belief. For always being there, not just for us, but for the whole world it seems, you are amazing and we love you.

With regard to the practical side of getting this book finished, thanks again to John Leathers, and to Julie Mellors, Derek Feasby, Julia Morgan, Carla Boulton and Sue Richardson. Also our thanks to Vera Feasby, whose generosity helped to make this book possible.

Finally, in the creation of this book, we must acknowledge and thank our Spirit Guides and connection with 'them upstairs' whom we know inspired much of it. At times when we couldn't quite find our words, we know 'they' willingly took up the reins and helped us on our way, enabling 'their' words to be heard. This brings a whole new meaning to the term 'ghost writers'!

ABOUT SPREADING THE MAGIC

Started in 2005 by Helen Leathers, 'Spreading The Magic' began life as an online resource for personal, spiritual and psychic development. Courses and workshops and a small range of products were available. Helen was also writing and had a number of projects on the go at once. But she knew it was extremely difficult to get an agent or publisher in the literary world. So she decided to create what she wanted and pull the two concepts together turning 'Spreading The Magic' into a publisher for her and Diane's specialist books on the spiritual side of life.

'Spreading The Magic' is a vehicle with which we seek to help others find and develop their own spirituality and integrating it into their daily life.

Our core values are open-mindedness and acceptance.

We want everyone to find their own path and know their own truth. To find the magic in themselves and to see it in others.

The 'magic' is our connection with life, our oneness with the universe and everything within it.

Through our courses, workshops, articles, books, products, websites and events we aim:
- To encourage, inform and inspire
- To simplify and demystify the unknown
- To open hearts and minds
- To promote non-judgement, acceptance and understanding
- To transform and enlighten
- To leave a positive impact
- To teach others to create their reality
- To raise consciousness, personally, socially and globally
- To remember
- To be
- To spread the magic

Become part of the change at www.spreadingthemagic.com

OTHER BOOKS & PRODUCTS

THE SPIRITUAL & PSYCHIC DEVELOPMENT WORKBOOK – A BEGINNERS GUIDE

Helen Leathers & Diane Campkin

An introduction to the theory and practical basics of spiritual and psychic work. This book will facilitate an opening up to and development of your natural spiritual and psychic abilities. This is the book we've been waiting for for years! RRP £9.95

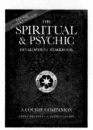

THE SPIRITUAL & PSYCHIC DEVELOPMENT WORKBOOK – A COURSE COMPANION

Helen Leathers & Diane Campkin

An in-depth course book for workshop leaders, development groups or just a bunch of like-minded friends. A step-by-step guide to running a group, circle or series of workshops on spiritual & psychic development. You don't have to think about it, we've done all the planning for you.

'With these workbooks we will walk and talk you through the process of discovering and developing your own natural abilities.'

This workbook is only available direct from Spreadng The Magic. Please take a look at our website for more details.

A4 Spiral Bound for ease of use. £19.95 + P&P

BRIGHT BLESSINGS

Spiritual Thoughts, Inspirational Quotes and Philosophical Observations on Life. By Helen Leathers

Ever wonder about the bigger picture and the spiritual side of life? Do you need inspiration? Are you happy? Do you truly know who you are and where you're heading?

This is a collection of articles, observations and quotes which aim to make you stop and think. Whether you need inspiration, a quiet moment, a focus for meditation, spiritual or philosophical advice or support, or maybe something different to do this weekend, this is the book to have within easy reach.

RRP £5.95

Register for updates and offers on these and find out about future products at: www.thepsychicworkbook.com or www.stmpublishing.co.uk

QUICK ORDER FORM

If you would like any additional copies of this book, or any of our other publications you can:

Buy Online at www.stmpublishing.co.uk

Buy Mail Order – Send this form and appropriate payment to:
Spreading the Magic, Tryfan, Barn Lane, Church Stretton, Shropshire, England SY6 6EB

Please send me .... copies of 'Help! I Think I Might Be Psychic' (£7.95 each)

Please send me .... copies of 'Bright Blessings' (£5.95 each)

Please send me .... copies of 'The Spiritual & Psychic Development Workbook -
A Beginners Guide' (£9.95 each)

P&P (UK)	£2.00 for first book	£1.00 for each subsequent book
P&P (Europe)	£2.50 for first book	£1.50 for each subsequent book
P&P (Rest of World)	£4.00 for first book	£3.00 for each subsequent book

Number of copies: Help! I Think I Might Be Psychic		x £7.95	£
Number of copies: Bright Blessings		x £5.95	£
Number of copies: SPDW A Beginners Guide		x £9.95	£
Postage for your region for first book:	£	x 1	£
Postage for your region for subsequent books:	£	x number of subsequent copies	£
TOTAL:			£

I enclose a cheque for £........................ (sterling only please) made payable to 'SPREADING THE MAGIC'.

YOUR DETAILS:

NAME: ....

ADDRESS:...

....

....

POSTCODE: .... COUNTRY: ....

TEL NO: .... EMAIL: ....

Please send more FREE information on:

☐ Other Books & Products ☐ Courses, Workshops, Seminars & Events
☐ By Email ☐ By Post

We aim to get your books to you within 7 working days of receiving your order, but it may take up to 28 working days, especially if you are ordering from outside of the U.K. Thank you for your patience.

Lightning Source UK Ltd.
Milton Keynes UK
30 November 2010

163672UK00003B/168/P